A GUIDE TO CATERING

*CATERING YOUR OWN EVENTS
OR
HIRING PROFESSIONALS*

BY DONNA MILLER

DJ'S GUIDES
P.O. Box 06472
Portland, OR 97206

Copyright ©1986 by Donna J. Miller. All rights reserved. No part of this book may be reproduced or transmitted in any form or by any means, electronic or mechanical, including recording, photocopying or by any information storage and retrieval system without the written permission of Donna J. Miller and DJ's Guides, P.O. Box 06472, Portland, Oregon 97206. U.S.A.

Reviewers may quote brief passages in connection with a review written for inclusion in a magazine, periodical, newspaper, or broadcast.

This edition is an expansion and revision of a work previously published as DJ's Guide To Catering, published by DJ's Guides, Copyright © 1984 by Donna J. Miller.

Second printing May 1986

Printed and bound in the United States of America.

ISBN # 0-9615919-0-0

Notice: The information in this book is true to the best of my knowledge. All recommendations are made without guarantees on the part of the author. The author disclaims all liability incurred in connection with the use of this information.

*This book is dedicated to
my daughter Tina,
whose love and understanding
has helped me more than
she will ever know.*

TABLE OF CONTENTS

Preface 6
Introduction: How to Use This Book 7

CHAPTER 1
    Outline 9-12

CHAPTER 2
    Number of Guests 14
    Type of Function: Party, Birthday, Anniversary, Graduation 14
    Church, Open House, Reunion 15
    Dinner, Barbecue & Picnic, Costume and Wedding Reception 16
    Wedding Section: Wedding Schedule, Who Pays? and Cakes 17-20

CHAPTER 3
    Set-Up 22
    Style 23

CHAPTER 4
    Budget 25
    Facility 25-26

CHAPTER 5
    Menus 28-32

CHAPTER 6
    Recipes 34-74
    Freezer Storage 75

CHAPTER 7

  Beverage 77-85
  Wine Information 78-85
  Bar Set-Up & Beverage Quantities 85

CHAPTER 8

  Invitations 87
  Decorations 87-88
  Rental Items 89-90
  Staff 91

CHAPTER 9

  Photographer 93
  Transportation 93
  Entertainment 93

CHAPTER 10

  Record Keeping 95-98
  Prologue 99
  Book Order Form 100

INDEX

PREFACE

After many years in the catering and food service industry, I concluded that there was a desperate need for a guide to help people plan and cater their own functions.

I developed **"A Guide to Catering"** to show you how to organize, determine costs, prepare foods, hire staff or caterers for various events. You will find step-by-step instructions, menus, recipes and much, much more to help you successfully complete your event.

This book contains many professional secrets. The intent of this book is to assist those who cannot afford a caterer or to instruct those who wish to hire professionals.

Whether you are planning a function to be catered by professionals or plan to cater yourself, this guide will aid you from start to finish in easy-to-read outlines and instructions that even the amateur entertainer can follow and understand.

Throughout this book you will find cost estimates to help you determine what type of overall budget is needed for many styles of functions. As costs vary in different areas, these estimates are designed to give you an approximate cost factor.

No matter if you are having a small or large event, you will find detailed information to help you through all phases involved in the planning, organizing, execution and completion of your event.

I hope that you will have as much fun using **"A Guide to Catering"** as I had in researching and writing it. Don't be afraid to experiment with different ideas or menus and remember to have a good time and enjoy your event as much as your guests. Good luck with all your entertaining.

INTRODUCTION: HOW TO USE THIS BOOK

The outline on pages 9-12 will help you plan and organize your particular event. This guide may be used for all types of functions, large or small. Simply make a rough outline of your event, using the outline in this book as a guide. If some details are undecided, continue on to the next topic; you will be able to get an estimate of the time and cost involved even if your event is in the early planning stages.

You will find explanations and instructions of each topic in the chapters following the outline. It is important to read this book entirely before starting an event, especially a large one. You may overlook something and the instructions will help you make some very important planning decisions.

Styles of events depend largely on your budget. It isn't necessary to go bankrupt in order to entertain in style. Most large events cost hundreds or thousands of dollars; by using this guide, you can find many ways to make your special occasion less expensive.

One very important decision to make concerns the location of the function. If you plan to rent a public or private facility, reserve the facility as early as possible. Some facilities are booked a year or more in advance, while others can be procured with a few months notice. Make sure your facility will accommodate the number of guests you plan to invite.

The menus and recipes included in this book are suggestions only; these are recipes that have worked well in the catering business, particularly for large events. You might want to add some of your favorite recipes. The menus will give you a guide to what types of foods to serve for different styles of events.

If you are hiring a professional caterer, please have your outline completed so you will not waste time discussing whats, whens and wheres. Ask the caterer if they have a list of food and supply items they can send to you before you decide on a menu. This will give you an idea of what a particular caterer has to offer. Other professionals might include restaurant and hotel Banquet and/or Catering Managers.

Once you have made these first major decisions, the remaining steps will fall into place. Complete your outline and make any necessary changes or adjustments. Throughout this guide you will find understandable tips to saving time and money, making your event easier to produce. Simply follow the instructions and soon you will be entertaining like a professional.

Chapter 10 contains a special form for recording important phone numbers and addresses. Use the blank pages within this book to keep records of additional information such as guest lists, decorating tips, new recipes, etc. You will be surprised how often you refer to the information you collect.

CHAPTER 1

OUTLINE

The most frequent mistake made by novice entertainers is poor planning. Avoid this problem by using the following outline to plan and organize your event.

There are no set rules for any given occasion. Many functions that previously required formal attire have become casual today. The key to any event is to make your guests feel comfortable, so plan accordingly.

OUTLINE
Planning A Function

A. NUMBER OF GUESTS
 1. Very small (under 25)
 2. Small (25-50)
 3. Moderate (50-100)
 4. Large (100-250)
 5. Very large (over 250)

B. TYPE OF FUNCTION
 1. Party
 2. Birthday
 3. Anniversary
 4. Graduation
 5. Church
 6. Open house
   a. Office
   b. Home
 7. Reunion
   a. Family
   b. School
 8. Dinner
 9. Barbecue & picnic
   a. Company picnic
   b. Family or friends
 10. Costume
 11. Wedding reception

C. TYPE OF SET-UP
 1. Snack or casual (no plate)
 2. Buffet
   a. Light hors d'oeuvres or finger food (no plate)
   b. Hearty hors d'oeuvres (plate w/picks or flatware)
   c. Light buffet meal (plate and flatware)
   d. Hearty buffet meal (plate and flatware)
 3. Sit down dinner
   a. Plate service: prepared in kitchen on plates and served by staff to each guest
   b. French service: prepared in kitchen on platters and served to each guest by staff
   c. American service: prepared in kitchen on platters and passed so each guest serves themselves
 4. Barbecue or picnic
 5. Cake or dessert only with or without beverage
 6. Beverage only
 7. Other

D. STYLE OF FUNCTION
    1. Casual
        a. Very
        b. Semi
    2. Formal
        a. Very
        b. Semi
    3. Other
        a. Special dress requirements

E. BUDGET
    1. Modest
    2. Moderate
    3. Unlimited
    4. Fund raiser or limited

F. LOCATION OF FUNCTION
    1. Home
    2. Church
    3. Rented hall or auditorium
    4. Office
    5. Club
    6. Outdoors
        a. Yard
        b. Park
    7. Other

G. MENU
    1. Casual
        a. Snack
        b. Hors d'oeuvres
        c. Pot luck
        d. Luncheon
        e. Light dinner
        f. Full dinner
        g. Cake or dessert
        h. Beverage
    2. Buffet
        a. Light
        b. Brunch
        c. Luncheon
        d. Light dinner
        e. Full dinner
    3. Sit down
        a. Casual
        b. Formal or gourmet
        c. Courses
        d. Other

H. BEVERAGE
   1. Non alcoholic
      a. Punch
      b. Coffee and/or tea
      c. Special drinks
      d. Soda pop
      e. Other
   2. Beer
      a. Bottle
      b. Keg

   3. Wine
      a. Champagne
      b. Punch
      c. Special drinks
   4. Liquor
      a. Punch
      b. Bar set-up
      c. Special drinks
   5. Other

I. INVITATIONS
   1. Printed or purchased
      a. Casual
      b. Formal
   2. Mailed or hand delivered
   3. Phone invitations
   4. Other

J. DECORATIONS
   1. Casual
   2. Formal
      a. Extensive or special decorations
   3. Flowers & plants
      a. Centerpiece
      b. Several arrangements
      c. Entire function
   4. Other

K. RENTAL ITEMS
   1. Supplies
      a. Paper (purchased)
      b. China and/or silver
      c. Glassware
      d. Linens (white or color)
      e. Tables (banquet, card, round)
      f. Chairs (wood or metal)

2. Special items
    a. Portable bar
    b. Barbecue
    c. Canopy
    d. Wedding items
3. Other

L. STAFF
1. Bartender
2. Servers
3. Kitchen help
4. Clean-up and or set-up
5. Other

M. PHOTOGRAPHER
1. Wedding reception
2. Videotape
3. Other

N. TRANSPORTATION
1. Limosine
2. Other

O. ENTERTAINMENT
1. Live music
    a. Band or orchestra
    b. Piano
2. Stereo or tapes
3. Other

P. RECORD KEEPING
1. Telephone numbers/addresses
2. Contracts
3. Licenses and permits
4. Any information that will help you complete your event

Now that you have outlined your event you should be able to see what is needed to complete the entire function. Read each chapter carefully and make notations as you go along. This will make final decision making much easier.

CHAPTER 2

NUMBER OF GUESTS
TYPE OF FUNCTIONS
WEDDING SECTION

Do not rely too heavily on the response to an R.S.V.P. request. Some people simply will not commit themselves one way or another.

It would be impossible to include examples of every type of function in this chapter. You will find information about the most common types of events in the following pages.

Number of Guests

Many people like to plan large events, inviting from 100 to 200 guests or more. This can be very expensive and time-consuming. If your budget is limited, reduce your cost by cutting the guest list.

It is hard to determine the number of people who will attend a function from a given guest list. You may want to request an R.S.V.P. on the invitation. This is a French term which translates to "respond if you please". You may want to go one step further and add the term "regrets only". Keep in mind that this procedure is not always reliable in getting an accurate guest count. If you are planning a small get together, simply call your guests on the telephone and ask if they will be attending.

Many factors should be considered when estimating the number of guest responses; for instance, weather, time of day, holidays, distance of travel, style of event and age of guests invited. As a rule approximately 50% to 70% of invited guests attend an event. You will have to make this estimate from all information collected prior to your event.

Type of Function

Party: You need not have a special reason to entertain a large or small group. Some people throw a party at the drop of a hat while others need a specific reason or occasion in order to entertain. If you are planning a casual party in your home or office you will want to keep foods to a minimum. Trays that can be prepared in advance and placed out at party time is the procedure easiest to follow. If you would like to be more formal or elaborate, a buffet might be in order. Remember that the more foods you serve the more work will be involved. Always consider the kitchen area when planning a large event. Do not take on more than this area will handle.

Birthday: Most birthday parties include cake and beverage service. You may want to hold your birthday party outside and plan a barbecue with the cake as dessert. The possibilities are endless for birthday styles, depending on whether the party is for an adult or a child. If you are having a surprise birthday you might want to tell the birthday person that you are having some type of event other than a birthday so that it will not look suspicious when you bring home invitations, food, decorations, etc. Plan to have some sort of entertainment or music. Check your phone book yellow pages for entertainers in your area.

Anniversary: The style of an anniversary party will depend on the year to be celebrated. If it is a 25th or 50th anniversary you may need some special arrangements. For instance, exchanging wedding vows, a photographer, videotape, special cake, formal wear or extra chairs for elderly people should be considered. Most family members will be happy to help you with the preparation or planning of an anniversary party. The most important thing to consider is the anniversary couple. Do not plan an event that would make them feel uncomfortable. Check what their wishes might be on this matter before planning such an event. Many anniversary parties are set up similarly to wedding receptions.

Graduation: Most graduation parties are for family members or close friends of the graduate. Many times a summer party is planned before a person leaves for college. Whatever the age of the graduate, you will need to consider what they might want in the way of a party. Many times mom and dad have good intentions, but a disaster may be the result. When planning food, remember the ages of the guests invited. It is best to serve foods that are liked by all ages.

Church: You will probably have all the help you can use if you are planning a function for your church. Church members usually jump right in and help with these events. If you are using the church kitchen, you will have a much easier time preparing foods than if you had to prepare in your kitchen and transport the items to the church. Most church functions are "pot luck" events. This makes planning much easier than making all the food yourself. Make a record of what most people are bringing and you should get a good idea of what extra items may be needed in order to round out the menu.

Open House: An office open house is sometimes very complicated to organize. If you do not have a refrigerator, you will have to bring ice and coolers to keep some items cold. If you do not have a stove or microwave, you will have to bring a small hot plate or warming divice. These are important things to consider when you are planning this type of event. One item usually overlooked is restroom facilities. Many office buildings are not built to accommodate large numbers of people. Also, fire regulations may limit the number of people. Notify security people that you will be having an open house in your office after hours. Parking is another thing to consider. Instruct people where available parking is located or how late parking is allowed in a particular area.

When planning an open house in your home you will have less to worry about, but you still will have a great deal of work to do. This type of event is best dealt with on a casual basis. Many times a "pot luck" open house or house warming can be a nice way to meet new neighbors. Usually a close friend or neighbor will help to organize an open house. Keep things as simple as possible. If you are meeting new neighbors, you will want to have time to get acquainted.

Reunions: Family reunions are usually planned every year for the same place and same time. Everyone knows in advance and can plan accordingly. Family reunions seem to be "pot luck" functions. If you are planning the event, it is important to know what everyone is bringing. You may want to tell people to bring specific items so you know what your menu will be in advance. For the most part, no one goes away from a family reunion hungry, no matter what menu is served. A large barbecue is always a good way to celebrate a family reunion. Have everyone bring salads and condiments and you provide the barbecued meats. What is important is that you see your relatives and have a good time. Plan games and activities for the children.

When planning school reunions keep in mind that some people may live out of town, or, for that matter, out of the country. Allow enough time for invitations to reach people. Place an ad in the local paper some months in advance for people who may not receive an invitation. You will need to start planning for these reunions as much as one year in advance. It may have been decided some years before to have a committee plan the reunion. For the most part, these functions are held at local restaurants or hotels, cost large sums, and tend to be the same. If you have a caterer handle your reunion and rent a hall you will probably spend less than you would at a restaurant. If you organize the reunion and do all the food yourself you can save a great deal of money and have a good time doing it. Be different and plan your reunion in your own style. Many times people have a family picnic the day following a dinner dance event. Whatever you decide, remember the object is to see people you haven't seen in many years.

Dinners: Large dinner parties can be very difficult to plan and run on schedule. There are many things to consider and nearly everything must be almost perfect. Serving is difficult; more servers are usually needed. "Sit down" dinners are demanding and will usually cost the most money. Buffets are somewhat easier but still require much time and help. Theme style dinners are very popular. These are sometimes pot luck. If you are serving in courses, make sure you have extra help. Plan your dinner around what the guests will enjoy most. Keep foods as simple as possible; do not prepare too many exotic or spicy dishes. You may desire to serve one or two complicated items; do not go beyond that unless you are planning a small dinner party and have more time for preparation.

Barbecues & Picnics: Company picnics can be expensive. It is possible for a company to spend thousands of dollars for an informal employee get together. With economic cutbacks, it has been necessary for some businesses to discontinue these special events. It is still possible to have an inexpensive event if, for example, some of the staff members plan and organize a pot luck. Or, arrange to have the employees bring salads and desserts and the company can supply the main course and paper supplies.

When planning a picnic for family or friends, it is most common to have a pot luck. With a little imagaination and hard work, it is possible to have a first class event for very little cost. For example, you can buy salads in large quantities from wholesalers and save a great deal of preparation time. You will have to check to find where to buy wholesale foods. You may want to plan a box lunch picnic in a park or by a lake. This will take some advance planning and preparation in order to box up all the lunches, and, if necessary to keep them cool. Regardless of style, outdoor functions seem to be very successful.

Costume: Halloween is probably the most obvious date on which to have a costume party. You can also have theme parties at other times of the year. Christmas, New Years Eve, Thanksgiving, 4th of July and Birthdays are just a few holidays celebrated with costume style parties. When giving an ethnic flavored event, ask guests to dress in the costume of that country, i.e., Mexican, Oriental, Hawaiian, French, German, Italian, etc. Plan menus according to traditional dishes of a particular country. This type of event can be a great deal of fun for all ages.

Wedding Receptions: This is probably the most difficult type of function to plan and execute. Besides the large number of guests, you will also need to consider many small details that are not necessary for other types of events. If you plan your reception using the outline in this book, you will cover almost every detail needed. It is most important to plan ahead when organizing an event as important as a wedding. Careful planning will produce a successful event. Make sure you book your facility far in advance. Have several people helping in the planning and preparation. It is usually better to hire people to help serve food & drink and let your friends and relatives enjoy the reception.

You can plan almost any style of reception imaginable. If you are having an early wedding, you may want to serve a brunch or luncheon buffet. If the wedding is in the late afternoon or evening, you may want to serve a dinner or simply light hors d'oeuvres. You will find many types of menus and recipes in the book to help you plan your reception. Do not feel that you have to serve a large dinner to your guests. Consider having only cake and beverage for your reception. Weddings can be very expensive and time-consuming. Reading this book in its entirety will enable you to find many ways to cut costs and make your job much more enjoyable. The next four pages are designed to help you better plan your reception. You will need to adapt this information to fit your particular needs.

WEDDING SCHEDULE

Six to twelve months before the Wedding:

Send engagement announcement to newspaper
Set the date
Determine wedding budget
Choose size, style and location of wedding
Choose size, style and location of reception
Make reservations for wedding and reception locations
Visit clergyman with your fiancée
Select wedding attendants
Select and order dresses and accessories, bride and bridesmaids
Select music for ceremony and reception
Start your guest list; finacée also starts his
Select photographer
Plan your new home; begin shopping for household

Three months before:

Guest lists should be completed
Order invitations, announcements and thank you's
Start shopping for your trousseau
Address annoucements and invitations
Arrange to see your doctor
Meet with caterer to consider reception details
Order wedding cake, cake boxes
Plan and make reservations for honeymoon
Advise mothers of colors for dresses
Select and order wedding rings
Select florist and order flowers

Two months before:

Make appointment with hairdresser
Register china, silver, crystal selections
Purchase a bride's register box to record gifts
Make arrangements for rehearsal dinner
Select wedding album, guest books and photo album
Order cake knife, server, ring pillow, garter, etc.
Choose and order gifts for attendants

One month before:

    Mail wedding invitations
    Have wedding portrait taken-prints for newspaper
    Check newspapers for announcement requirements
    Plan party for bridesmaids
    Plan party for groomsmen
    Final fitting of dresses
    Write thank you notes as gifts are received

Two weeks before:

    Send annoucements and photo to newspapers
    Get marriage license
    Arrange transportation to church
    Arrange rehearsal-inform all concerned
    Determine rehearsal dinner and reception seating
    Complete your trousseau
    Write thank you notes

One week before:

    Final check with photographer, florist, musician, etc.
    Bridesmaids' party-present them with gifts
    Groomsmens' party-groom presents them with gifts
    Give final guest count to caterer
    Prepare announcements-maid of honor mails day after wedding
    Begin packing for your honeymoon
    Continue to acknowledge gifts as received

WHO PAYS?

Bride's Parents:

Wedding invitations
Rent of hall or church
Rehearsal Dinner
Bridesmaids' bouquets
Flowers in the church
Gifts to the bridesmaids
Fees for sexton
Transportation of the bridal party to the church and reception
Bride's personal trousseau and her linen trousseau
Expenses of the reception, including hall rental, food, beverage, flowers, decorations, staff, entertainment, etc.

Attendants:

Their own transportation to bride's home
Their wedding costume
Their presents to bride and groom

Groom:

Engagement ring
Wedding ring
Marriage license
Bride's bouquet
Bachelor dinner
Ushers' gifts
Gift to bride
Boutonnieres for the best man and ushers
Contribution to the officiating clergyman
All the expenses of the wedding trip or honeymoon

Groom's Parents:

Their own wedding costume
Wedding present to newly married couple
Any entertaining they care to do in honor of the couple

CAKES

How to cut a wedding cake

A. Cut vertically through the bottom tier at the edge of the second tier as indicated by the dotted line marked 1. Then cut out wedge-shaped pieces as shown by 2.

B. When these pieces have been served, follow the same procedure with the middle tier. Cut vertically through the second tier at the edge of the top tier as indicated by dotted line 3. Then cut out wedge-shaped pieces as shown by 4.

C. When pieces from the second tier have been served, return to the bottom tier and cut along dotted line 5. Cut another row of wedged-shaped pieces as shown by 6.

D. The remaining tiers may be cut into the desired size pieces.

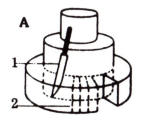 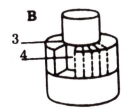 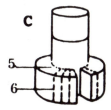 

Number of servings per double-layer cake tier

Serving size: ¾ inch slice, by 4 inches high, by 2 inches deep.

ROUND CAKES	SQUARE CAKES	HEART CAKES
8" - 32 servings	6" - 14 servings	6" - 12 servings
10" - 45 servings	8" - 32 servings	7" - 15 servings
12" - 65 servings	10" - 45 servings	9" - 28 servings
14" - 95 servings	12" - 60 servings	10" - 35 servings
16" - 103 servings	14" - 84 servings	12" - 48 servings
18" - 125 servings	16" - 105 servings	13" - 60 servings
	18" - 130 servings	15" - 90 servings

CHAPTER 3

SET-UP STYLE

The additional cost for using china, glassware and flatware will exceed $1.00 per place setting. By using plastic and/or styrofoam products, you will be able to cut your cost by as much as 80%.

Some people prefer creating their own style, while others feel more comfortable staying with traditional forms. Simply use good taste and common sense.

Set-Up

Today it is acceptable to use almost any style of set-up for an event. Determine the type of set-up appropriate for your function and with what you feel most comfortable.

There are many set-up variations. Usually space is the determining factor. If you will be using a facility with unlimited space, there are many set-up options available. If your facility is small, choose a set-up that will consume less space and allow your guests more room to enjoy themselves.

Most large events are set up using some sort of buffet style. Buffet merely means that the guests choose and serve foods themselves. If meat carving or special serving is required, you may need to position staff members to assist guests in dishing and serving. Buffets will require replenishing from time to time, so you will need extra staff members to keep things running smoothly. Do not set-up food serving tables too far from kitchen or preparation area.

If you would like to be more formal and serve a seated dinner, remember that tables and chairs will require a great deal of space, not to mention the additional cost involved. On a more casual note, you could serve light hors d'oeuvres and still have an elegant event.

Plates and flatware are very important in terms of set-up, menu, preparation and cost. You need to keep in mind that people will eat more if plates and flatware are used. On the other hand, if meal-type service is used, plates and flatware are a necessity.

Contrary to what some people think, it is acceptable to use small plates (six to seven inches) for buffet style meals. However, food items should be small enough to fit on the plate without falling over the edge.

There is one very important point that should be mentioned and there is no polite way in which to say it. Large events such as Wedding Receptions seem to bring out the worst in some people. They will eat like they haven't eaten in weeks and drink your bar dry. It is hard to say what causes this phenomenon but it can be embarrassing to you and your guests, especially when someone piles a plate so high with food that it defies gravity.

Some people are just not used to attending large functions and do not know that when you serve hors d'oeuvres or finger foods it might mean that no plates are used. Guests have been known to take plates from the cake table and place them on the food table simply because they felt that there should be plates there.

It is a good idea to have staff members guarding the tables so the well-meaning guests or relatives do not rearrange things, negating your hard work. There is no need to embarrass these people; merely have someone point out the procedure to be used.

If you plan to not serve your buffet items immediately as guests arrive, plan to separate the tables where the food will be served from the guests. If you have your supplies set up, someone will grab a plate and wait impatiently for you to serve them. If you can't close the tables off until you are ready to serve, station staff members near the food tables so that they can divert your guests until the food is ready.

You will be able to get help from caterers or other professionals concerning the best procedure for your event. Remember that this is your function and you will have the final say in all arrangements.

Style

Your budget, the location, the season, age of your guests, and the time of day will be the determining factors in deciding the style of your event. Most functions are casual to moderately formal.

If cost is your biggest concern, find ways to reduce supplies and decorations. These items can be just as costly as food and beverage. Purchasing items in advance can save a great deal of money.

Remember, the more formal your event, the more expensive it will be. You can have a stylish event without paying a fortune for it. Even an outdoor barbecue can be an elegant affair if the proper menu and decorations are used. This is why it is important to plan an outline in advance of any function. Outlines will show you just what is involved and where you can make needed changes. The style will depend largely on what is necessary to complete your event and what will make you feel most comfortable.

CHAPTER 4

BUDGET FACILITY

Where there is a will there is a way. If your budget is limited, don't worry. You will be able to have almost any style of event by using a little hard work and creative thinking. Always allow some overrun on the cost of your function. Most events will cost more than originally planned.

Many cities have limited large facilities available to the public. Some people find that they have planned an event but are unable to rent a place to have it. Popular facilities may be booked as much as two years in advance.

Budget

Probably the single most important factor in planning any type of event is the overall cost involved. You may need to revise your plans if you find you have exceeded your available budget when outlining the event. There are many ways to reduce and substitute when necessary.

If you plan your extravaganza far enough in advance, you may be able to buy some items ahead and spread your cost over a period of time and paydays. Such items as invitations, decorations, napkins, plates and other paper products can be purchased months in advance. Watch seasonal sales and buy when the prices are low. Space out your deposit payments so you do not pay large sums of money at one time.

Throughout the menu and recipe chapters of this book you will find estimates of catered food costs verses the cost of purchasing the foods yourself. Catering prices will vary, as well as the services provided by different caterers or businesses. Food costs are estimates only and should be regarded as such.

It is important to get at least three catering estimates before deciding on a caterer. Catering prices may seem like a great deal of money; however, remember that you are paying for the service of a professional when hiring a caterer.

Some caterers may add a 15% to 20% gratuity charge to the total bill. This is standard with restaurants and hotels. Ask for the total cost in advance so there will be no question as to what is owed after your function is completed.

Each caterer, restaurant or hotel has different requirements regarding payment and deposits. Usually a deposit is required to hold your booking date and assure the caterer or business that you will have your function as scheduled. This deposit can range from 10% to as much as 50% of the total costs, depending on the event and the time of year. Ask if your deposit is refundable if the event is cancelled or what other restrictions might apply. Caterers or Banquet Managers will be happy to discuss all the details with you before you sign contracts or make a final decision.

Facility

When choosing a location take into consideration cost, time of day, distance of travel, space, season, parking, work area or kitchen, and, last but not least, the restroom facilities.

You can save 40% to 75% of the cost by using common sense and hard work. Using a private home instead of a rented hall can save you considerable money. Bear in mind that if you hold your event outdoors, adequate room indoors might be needed in case of bad weather. You may want to erect canopies to shade your guests on hot, sunny days.

Check with the people in charge of a rented facility or park for requirements or limitations which might apply to your function. The items might include: length of use, electricity usage, alcoholic beverages, security persons, key deposit, damage deposit, insurance, licenses and special permits.

For a list of facilities in your area, check the yellow pages of your phone book under Halls and Auditoriums or Clubs and Organizations. Usually you will find many more facilities available than you have time to check out. You can also call your local Chamber of Commerce or Better Business Bureau for information on available facilities or businesses in your area.

Friends and relatives are very good sources of information about facilities. Not all are listed in the phone book and some are only rented to someone known by members or owners of these facilities. It pays to research all avenues when looking for an appropriate place to hold your function. Doing some easy detective work can uncover many great bargains.

Halls and auditoriums will cost between $100.00 to $700.00 as a rule. Some will be more, and you may find a facility free of charge or requiring a small donation. The factor here is who you know! Many facilities will require a deposit and/or a cleaning fee. Ask if these deposits and fees are refundable or applied to the cost of the facility.

Most parks are free of charge but some will require a permit or reservation. If a fee is required it is usually small and is merely to hold your reservation and pay for maintenance. Again, make sure you check all requirements and restrictions that may apply.

Restaurants and hotels are one option you may want to consider for a location. However, keep in mind that several limitations may apply when using such facilities. You will usually have only 2 or 3 food selections in a given price range and will be required to use only their services. You cannot bring in food or caterers to a restaurant or hotel facility. This is almost always a very strict regulation. The restaurant or hotel will be happy to discuss this matter in detail.

Alcoholic beverages are another consideration. You will have to use the restaurant or hotel's alcohol and they will attach a 10% to 20% gratuity to all beverage services. This can be a very costly item if you are having an open bar at your function. An "open bar" means that the host or hostess pays for all expenses. If you want to cut your cost consider having a "no host" bar. This means that the guests pay for the drinks they order from the bar. Check with local agencies to see if special licenses are required for your particular event.

Some caterers have access to non-public facilities and will include the facility charge in the total catering cost. Discuss this subject when you call for a list of available catered items.

No matter where you plan to have your function, see the facility before you commit yourself. Some may sound great over the phone but in the light of day many facilities leave something to be desired. Check restrooms to make sure they are clean and in good working order. Outside appearance is important, especially if the function is a daytime event.

If you have any questions about a business, call your local Better Business Bureau. Always ask for a receipt and do not sign a contract until you know exactly what you are signing.

Do not forget the clean-up of your facility. This usually is overlooked until the last minute. Plan ahead and have someone scheduled for this task. You will be too tired to push a broom after you have worked so hard to make your event a complete success. Also check to see if you get a refund for cleaning the facility.

Please take into consideration that some facilities are in residential neighborhoods. Noise travels at night, so be considerate of others.

CHAPTER 5

MENUS

Deciding on the proper menu requires a great deal of careful thought. Many people overdo it and plan more food than necessary. Very few plan too little food.

Usually five to six different food items is sufficient for most hors d'oeuvre or light buffet style functions. Allow a total of eight to twelve hors d'oeuvre pieces per person, depending on foods and type of event. When planning a buffet meal you will need more food per serving than a served meal, especially if guests will be serving themselves.

The menus in this chapter are suggestions only and may need to be adjusted to suit your needs.

Menu

Each event is different and you will have to make your food selections according to what will be best for your function. Each menu in this chapter will cover a different set-up and style of event. You may want to choose recipes from several menus in order to get the exact foods desired. Once you have decided on your style and set-up, the menu selection will depend largely on your **culinary skills and the overall budget**.

Depending on your culinary skills or expertise, you will want to choose the **recipes that will be the** easiest for you to follow and prepare. Donot over-extend yourself; allow enough time to complete every item before your guests are ringing the doorbell or walking through the door. This is a common mistake made by many newcomers to the catering business. Plan your time wisely and stick mostly to recipes you have used before or know are within your skill level.

The recipes in this book are for all levels of expertise. Be sure to read through each recipe completely so you understand what is involved in completing it. When you can, try to prepare items ahead and freeze them. You will find a chart on page 75 to give you an idea of how far in advance you can freeze some foods which may be on your menu.

For variety, select different textures, flavors, colors and temperatures of food. Most people like something familiar in the way of food, so don't overwhelm your guests with too many exotic or spicy foods.

When catering a function yourself, have qualified helpers assisting in the preparation. Do not try to do everything yourself. Have several friends or relatives assist organizing the event. It might be better to hire outside people for the day of the funciton so your friends or relatives can enjoy the event that they helped make so special.

If your budget is limited, keep the foods simple but nicely garnished. This will cut cost and also save you much time in preparation. Outline your menu in detail so you know how much time and work is involved.

When purchasing food yourself, prices will vary depending upon the season, geography and availability of items. You may be able to use frozen items when fresh items are not available. Watch sales and shop wisely and you will cut costs considerably.

The time of year will also determine the cost of foods. You will notice there is a substantial cost difference between doing the function yourself and hiring a professional to cater your event. Remember that the difference in cost means you will be doing all the work. It is hard to determine just what your time is worth in comparison to a professional caterer.

Caterers or Banquet Managers will assist you in planning menus that will suit your budget and needs. They will be happy to do what is possible to accommodate special requests for foods and service. Food prices will vary depending on whether you use a caterer, restaurant or hotel. Caterers will give you a price that does not include the room or facility. A restaurant or hotel will usually give you a cost that includes the charge for the room or facility. Ask for all charges involved when contacting either type of business.

Check thoroughly if a caterer or restaurant gives you a price that is a great deal lower than the other bids you received. This usually means one of two things; either they are inexperienced or are desperate and will take any job. Your best bet is to stick with a well-established firm when hiring a caterer or professional.

The following menus will give you an idea about the foods that work well for different styles and set-up. These menus can be mixed and matched as you see fit. No two functions are exactly the same and neither are menus. Incorporate some of your favorite recipes to create the menu you desire. Keep menus well rounded and don't serve too many of the same types of foods.

All costs mentioned in this chapter are estimates for food **only** and do not include supplies, staff, decorations, hall rental, etc. Some adjustments may be needed since prices will vary from city to city.

The following symbols are used for each recipe to give you an idea of the cost involved and the level of expertise needed to complete the recipe. If you purchase foods on sale you may be able to cut the original cost of the recipe by as much as 50%.

    ¢ = Inexpensive   S = Simple
    ¢$ = Moderate   E = Easy or moderately difficult
    $ = Expensive   D = Difficult or time-consuming
    $$ = Very Expensive   F = May be frozen

Menus & Style   Your Cost Catered Cost

#1 Hors d'oeuvre Style (without plate) $85-$120 $300-$450+
Based on 50 guests

  ¢$S Cheese Tray and/or Fruit Tray
  ¢DF Filo (phyllo) Pastries **or**
     Cocktail Puffs
  ¢$DF Rumaki **or** Pot Stickers
  ¢$E Salmon Spread
  ¢$EF Chicken Wings

#2 Hors d'oeuvre Style (with plate) $100-$175 $450-$750+
Based on 50 guests

  ¢$E Fresh Mushroom Dip
  ¢$E Pâté **or** Barbeque Pork
  $$E Barbecued Prawns **or**
     Baked Whole Salmon
  ¢$DF Cocktail Quiche
  ¢EF Dolmates **or** Spinach Balls
  ¢$E Chicken w/Bearnaise Sauce **or**
     Pasta Shells w/Bearnaise Sauce

#3 **Hors d'oeuvre Style (with plate)** $65-$85 $175-$300+
Based on 25 guests *Some caterers have*
All recipes may be frozen *minimum charges*

- ¢EF Spinach Balls
- ¢$EF Meatballs
- ¢$EF Cocktail Puffs
- ¢EF Dolmates **or** Rumaki
- ¢$EF Chicken Wings

#4 **Wine Tasting (without plate)** $35-$50 $100-$225+
Based on 25 guests *Some caterers have*
minimum charges

- ¢$S Cheese Tray and/or Fruit Tray
- ¢$E Pâté
- ¢S Breads and Crackers
- Coffee

#5 **Buffet Brunch** $75-$100 $250-$425+
Based on 25 guests

- ¢E Buffet Potatoes
- $E Glazed Ham & Sausage
- ¢$E Epicurean Chicken Livers
- ¢$E Cheese & Egg Scramble
- ¢$F Easy French Toast
- Fresh Fruit Juice & Coffee
- Muffins or Sweet Rolls

#6 **Buffet or Sit Down Luncheon** $200-$250 $900-$1,800+
Based on 100 guests

- ¢$E Fruit Tray
- ¢$E Salmon Spread and/or Pâté
- ¢$S Chinese Chicken Salad
- $EF Beef Burgundy
- $S Rice Pilaf
- ¢$E Banana Cake
- Rolls and butter
- Coffee and/or punch

#7 **Buffet or Sit Down Dinner** $200-$250 $750-$1,500+
Based on 75 guests

    ¢ $D   Chicken and Pork Pâté
    ¢ S   Tomato and Pepper Salad **or**
    ¢ $E   Mushroom, Bleu Cheese and Walnut Salad
    $$DF   Chicken and Crab Kiev w/Gruyere Sauce
    ¢ S   Rice Pilaf
    ¢ E   Gingered Carrots
    ¢ $E   Tomato Timbles
    ¢ E   Madeleines
    ¢ $EF   Creamed Chocolate **or** French Vanilla
          Ice Cream w/Grand Marnier
        Bread **or** Rolls and butter

#8 **Sit Down Dinner** $75-$90 $200-$300+
Based on 10 guests   *Some caters have minimum charges*

    $$E   Macadamia Prawns
    ¢ $E   Stuffed Mushrooms
    ¢ $E   Leek Soup **or**
        French Onion Soup
    ¢ $S   Sherbet and Champagne
    ¢ $E   Broccoli w/Bacon and Almonds
    ¢ S   Rice Pilaf
    $$E   Lamb w/Rosemary Stuffing **or**
    $$E   Chicken Breast w/Bearnaise Sauce
    ¢ $E   Vanilla Ice Cream w/Orange
          Cranberry Sauce
        Croissants and butter
        Coffee w/condiments: Whipped cream,
          brown sugar, shaved chocolate

#9 **Picnic, Barbecue or Pot Luck** $85-$110 $300-$400+
Based on 25 guests

    ¢ E   Spinach Dip **or** Guacomole
    ¢ $E   Salmon Spread
    $D   Barbecued Spareribs **or**
        Spinach Lasagne
    ¢ S   Grilled or Baked Garlic Bread
        Salad
        Dessert
        Beverage

The following menu is based on approximately 300 guests. Cost will vary depending on items served, set-up, style and time of year. Some items may be donated or purchased at reduced rates. Have several committees working on different stages of the event. This will help make things go more smoothly.

#10 Large Feast or Fund Raiser $175-$250 $1,500-$3,000+

    ¢$D Spaghetti Sauce
    ¢E Spaghetti Pasta
    ¢S Garlic Bread
    ¢S Tossed Salad w/dressing
    ¢$ Parmesan Cheese
          Dessert
          Beverage

All cost estimates in this book are based on 1986 prices. Many factors will determine the final costs. If you are using your own recipes, you will need to make cost estimates according to local prices.

Not all recipes are mentioned in the preceding menus. For a complete list of recipes refer to the index.

CHAPTER 6

RECIPES
FREEZER STORAGE

The following pages contain recipes mentioned in the previous menus. You can mix recipes to obtain the desired menu. Read all instructions carefully so you understand what is involved in completing each recipe. You may increase or decrease the servings of each.

You may wish to include several of your favorite recipes so that the menu fits your occasion.

Plan a menu outline to determine your preparation time. Some recipes are time consuming while others take only minutes to complete.

Preparing food items and storing them in the freezer will help cut down last minute preparation. Many foods can go from freezer to oven to table. Remember that not all foods can be frozen, so be careful.

Appetizers

Stuffed Mushrooms
Serves: 20-25

1 lb. mushrooms, small to medium sized
1 onion, chopped
¼ c. green pepper
½ of the mushroom stems, chopped fine
8 slices of bacon, cooked and drained

4 ozs. cream cheese, room temp.
½ c. grated cheddar cheese
Seasonings to taste: celery salt, garlic salt, curry, white pepper

Remove stems from mushrooms and chop ½. Rinse and dry mushrooms. Add butter to skillet and saute chopped onions, green pepper and stems until onions are transparent. Let cool slightly. In bowl mix onions, green pepper, stems and cream cheese. When well mixed add crumbled bacon and cheddar cheese. Season to taste. Stuff each mushroom with mixture (heaping). Place mushrooms in a buttered baking dish and bake at 350° F for 15 minutes or until mixture is melted. Watch closely so not to over cook. Serve hot. You may stuff mushrooms early in the day. Cover and refrigerate until ready to cook.

Fresh Mushroom Dip
Serves: 25

12 ozs. bacon
1 lb. fresh mushrooms, sliced
1 large red onion, chopped
2 cloves garlic, pressed
2 tbls. flour
8 ozs. cream cheese

2 tsp. Worcestershire sauce
2 tsp. soy sauce
½ to ⅔ c. sour cream
Salt and white pepper to taste
Bread sticks or crackers

Cook bacon until crisp, remove and drain on paper towel. Discard all but 1 tbls. bacon grease. Add onions and sauté for several minutes over medium heat. Add garlic and mushrooms, continue cooking until mushrooms **begin** to turn dark. Sprinkle flour over mushroom mixture and stir for one minute. Reduce heat to low and add cream cheese, Worcestershire sauce, soy sauce, salt and white pepper to taste. Stir until cream cheese is melted. Remove from heat and add sour cream. Stir in bacon. Serve warm with bread sticks or crackers. May be made ahead and refrigerated.

Spinach & Cheese Filo Pastries   Yields: 85-100

- 1 lb. filo pastry (or phyllo)
- ½ lb. unsalted butter, melted
- 1½ c. chopped spinach, cooked and well drained
- 1 c. Swiss or Gruyere cheese, grated
- ¼ c. Parmesan cheese, grated
- ¼ c. green onions, chopped
- 2 eggs
- ¼ tsp. onion salt
- ¼ tsp. garlic salt
- ¼ tsp. white pepper

Mix spinach, cheeses, onion, eggs, onion salt, garlic salt and white pepper in a food processor, blend together for 15-20 seconds. Do not over process. Place one sheet of filo on a flat work surface. Keep remaining filo covered with plastic or damp cloth, do not let filo become wet or dried out. Brush the sheet with melted butter, cut the sheet into four strips lengthwise approximately 2½ to 3 inches in width. Place a small amount of filling in the bottom corner of each strip. Fold corner over filling forming a triangle. Continue to fold filo in a triangle shape. Brush finished filo triangle with butter and place on a cookie sheet. Repeat with remaining filo. Completed filo triangles may be frozen or covered and placed in the refrigerator for up to 12 hours. To bake, preheat oven to 400° F. Bake 15 minutes or until golden brown. Serve immediately.

Substitute frozen spinach souffle for chopped spinach. Omit the eggs and adjust seasonings.

Liver pate makes a great filling for filos. Try other cheeses or meats, be creative.

Spinach Balls   Serves: 25

- 3½ lbs. frozen chopped spinach, thawed and well drained
- 2 c. seasoned bread crumbs
- 10 ozs. freshly grated Parmesan cheese
- 1 c. butter, melted
- 10 green onions, chopped
- 5-6 eggs, lightly beaten
- 2 tbls. Dijon mustard
- ¼ tsp. nutmeg
- ½ tsp. white pepper

Combine all ingredients in large bowl. Form into small 1-inch balls and place on an ungreased cookie sheet. Bake in a 350° F oven for 15 to 20 minutes or until lightly browned. Serve with Dijon mustard. Spinach balls may be frozen and heated before serving.

Spinach Dip
Serves: 25

- 2 packages frozen spinach, thawed, well drained, chopped
- 8 ozs. cream cheese, soft
- 1 package dry leek soup mix
- ½ c. chopped green onion
- 2 cloves garlic, pressed
- Sour cream
- Salt and white pepper to taste

Mix spinach, cream cheese, leek soup mix, onions and garlic in food processor until blended. Add sour cream until desired consistency. Season with salt and pepper to taste. Serve with french bread or crackers.

Serving suggestion: Hollow out the inside of a large loaf of bread. Place spinach dip inside and cut hollowed bread into chunks.

Meatballs
Serves: 25-30

- 5 lbs. Hamburger
- 1½ c. seasoned bread crumbs
- 5 eggs, lightly beaten
- ½ to ⅔ c. milk
- ½ tsp. onion powder
- 1 tsp. garlic salt
- ½ tsp. white pepper
- Other seasoning optional

Combine all ingredients in large bowl. Form into small 1-inch balls and place on an ungreased cookie sheet. Bake in a 375° F oven for 15 to 20 minutes, check for doneness. Serve with your favorite sauce.

Hot Crab Dip
Yields: 2 c.

- 6 oz. crabmeat
- ½ c. sour cream
- 3 oz. cream cheese, room temp.
- 1 tbls. lemon juice
- 1 tsp. prepared horseradish
- 2 tbls. minced green pepper
- 1 tbls. minced pimento
- Dash Worcestershire sauce

Drain crabmeat; set aside. In a medium saucepan, combine sour cream, cream cheese, lemon juice and horseradish, stirring to blend. Add green pepper, pimento, Worcestershire and crabmeat. Stir over low heat until bubbly. Serve with French bread or crackers.

Crab Dip
Yields: 3 c.

- 1 c. mayonnaise
- ½ c. sour cream
- 1 garlic clove, pressed
- 1 tbls. dry sherry
- 1 tbls. minced fresh parsley
- 1 tbls. capers, rinsed, drained
- 1 tbls. green onions, minced
- 2 tsp. fresh lemon juice
- 1 tsp. chives
- 1 tsp. Worcestershire Sauce
- ½ tsp. salt
- ⅛ tsp. ground red pepper
- 12 oz. crabmeat, rinsed, drained and tossed with 2 tbls. lemon juice
- Crackers and assorted breads

Combine all ingredients except crabmeat and crackers in a medium bowl and mix well. Gently stir in crabmeat. Cover and refrigerate at least four hours. Serve with crackers and breads.

Crab & Swiss on Sourdough
Serves: 10-12

- 6 oz. crabmeat
- 1 c. grated Swiss cheese
- ½ c. sour cream
- 2 tbls. minced green onions
- 1 tbls. lemon juice
- ½ tsp. Worcestershire sauce
- ¼ tsp. salt
- 1 can waterchestnuts, sliced, drained
- Sourdough bread

Drain crabmeat. In a small bowl, combine crabmeat, cheese, sour cream, onions, lemon juice, Worcestershire sauce and salt; set aside. Finely chop chestnuts; add to crabmeat mixture. Preheat oven to 400° F. Slice bread into one inch slices. Spread about one tablespoon of mixture evenly over each slice of bread. Top with small slice of waterchestnut. Arrange on a cookie sheet. Bake 10-15 minutes until bubbly and slightly browned. Serve hot.

Cheese Tray

Arrange large wedges or wheels of cheeses on a large platter. Allow the guests to cut their own servings. This appears more elegant and is very simple to prepare. Choose cheeses of different colors and textures. Cheese trays should be colorful and served cold if possible.

Guacamole
Serves: 25

4 large ripe avocados	2 cloves garlic, pressed
2 large ripe tomatoes	½ tsp. celery salt
¾ c. chopped green onions	½ tsp. garlic salt
½ c. chunky salsa	¼ tsp. white pepper
½ c. sour cream	Tabasco sauce to taste
¼ c. cooked, crumbled bacon	Grated cheddar cheese (opt.)

In a food processor, mix avocados until smooth. Cut tomatoes into small chunks, reserve half. Place ½ of the tomatoes in the food processor with avocados. Add onions, salsa, sour cream, bacon, garlic, celery salt, pepper and tabasco, blend until just mixed. Place in large serving bowl, mix in remaining tomato chunks and garnish with grated cheddar cheese if desired. Serve with tortilla chips. Sour cream will slow darkening of avocado.

Mexican Platter
Serves: 25

2½ c. spicy refried beans	1 c. sour cream
1½ to 2 lbs. lean hamburger, cooked and drained	¾ c. chunky green salsa
½ lb. cheddar cheese, grated	¾ c. chunky red salsa
½ lb. jack or swiss cheese, grated	1 c. fresh tomatoes, chopped
½ lb. smoked gouda, grated	Jalapeno peppers (opt.)
1 c. green onion, chopped	Chopped black olives (opt.)
2 c. guacamole or chopped avocado (ripe)	Mexican chips

On a large platter, spread refried beans. Sprinkle cooked meat over beans. Spread guacamole over meat. Mix three cheeses in a large bowl. Sprinkle ⅓ of the cheese mixture over the salsas. Spread sour cream over cheeses. Top with tomatoes, remaining green onions and cheeses. Garnish with Jalapeno peppers and chopped back olives.

You may layer the ingredients in any order you wish. Make sure that your platter is large enough to hold all the ingredients. You can make this platter early in the day and refrigerate until needed.

Variation: Use cooked chicken meat or left-over turkey meat. Pork is also a good substitute for beef.

Cocktail Quiche

Yields: 75-100 pieces per sheet

5 c. grated Swiss cheese
2 c. chopped green onions
2 lbs. bacon, cooked and crumbled
1 qt. ½ & ½
12 eggs

1 tsp. nutmeg
½ tsp. celery salt
½ tsp. granulated garlic
½ tsp. salt
¼ tsp. white pepper

Perfect Pie Crust

4 c. flour
1 tbls. sugar
2 tsp. salt
1 large egg

1¾ c. vegetable shortening
1 tbls. vinegar
½ c. water
2 large cookie sheets w/sides (11 x 17)

Pie crust: Mix flour, salt and sugar in large bowl. Add shortening and blend with fork until mixture is crumbly. In small bowl mix together water, egg and vinegar. Pour liquid into flour mixture. Stir with fork until mixture is doughlike. Divide dough into two portions and shape into balls. Wrap in plastic and chill at least 1 hour. May be refrigerated for four days or frozen for one month. When ready to bake quiche, take dough from refrigerator and let set for 10 minutes. On floured board, roll out dough to fit the cookie sheet. This takes some practice. Piece together if needed. Then fold the dough several times so you can lift it into the cookie sheet. Unfold the dough and make sure the dough goes all the way up the sides of the sheet (like you were making a pie shell) and leaving some to over-hang the top. Cut off the excess dough and scallop the edges. Repeat with the second cookie sheet. Take half of the cheese, onions and bacon and spread evenly over the bottom of the dough shell. Repeat with second sheet. Place ½ & ½, eggs, nutmeg, celery salt, garlic, salt and pepper in a blender (if this won't all fit, do ½ at a time) and mix until well blended. Pour ½ of this mixture into each shell (over dry ingredients) just covering the cheese, onion and bacon. Do not fill too full. If more liquid is needed, add enough milk to cover the dry ingredients. Place cookie sheets in oven and bake at 350° F for 45 minutes or until top of quiche is golden brown (do not overcook). Remove from oven and let rest for several minutes. Cut into desired number of pieces and serve as soon as possible. Quiche may be prepared to the stage of adding the liquid and refrigerated overnight. You may wish to freeze the prepared pie shell in the cookie sheet. Just thaw and add ingredients. Left-over cooked quiche may be reheated.

Spinach Quiche: Thaw and drain three small boxes of frozen chopped spinach. Remove all liquid. Take 5 cups of grated Swiss cheese, ½ c. grated Parmesan cheese, 2 c. chopped green onions, 1 tsp. nutmeg, ½ tsp. granulated garlic, ½ tsp. celery salt, ½ tsp salt and ¼ tsp. white pepper and divide between two dough shells as above. Bake for 40-45 minutes. Do not overcook. Cut and serve as soon as possible.

Cocktail Puffs

Yields: 60-65

1 c. water	4 eggs
½ c. butter	Pinch of salt
1 c. flour	

Place water and butter in medium saucepan and bring to boil. Remove from heat and add flour. Stir until flour is formed into a ball (leaving sides of pan). Let cool for several minutes. Add one egg at a time, mixing after each egg. Place a small blob (about 1 tsp.) of mixture on an ungreased cookie sheet and bake in a 400° F oven until browned. Slit each puff and let cool before filling. You may freeze unfilled puffs. Bring frozen puffs to room temperature before filling. Once puffs are filled, serve at once.

Filling

¾ c. cooked, chopped meat, poultry or seafood	3 to 4 ozs. cream cheese, room temp.
	2 tbls. green onion, chopped
¼ tsp. celery salt	¼ tsp. garlic salt
Dash curry (opt.)	Sliced almonds (opt.)

Mix together all ingredients. Fill each puff with small amount of mixture. Do not use fillings that are runny or puffs will get soggy.

Pasta Shells w/Bearnaise sauce: Use filling above to stuff cooked pasta (large sea shells). When filled, place in baking dish and top with Bearnaise sauce. You may also use the spinach filling from the spinach and cheese filo recipe. To serve, bake in a 350° F oven for 15 minutes. Filled shells may be frozen without sauce.

Fruit Tray

Arrange large platters of fresh fruits. Decorate the trays with lettuce, parsley, fresh mint, etc. If you wish to serve a dipping sauce, mix brown sugar and sour cream together until desired flavor is obtained. You may want to cut fruit in advance. Place cut fresh fruit in airtight plastic bags. You can cut most fruit early in the day providing you handle carefully. Some fruit should be cut at the last minute. Get serving and decorating ideas by looking through your cook books or magazines. Fresh pineapple is always a favorite fruit. Pour a small amount of Creme de Menthe over the fresh pineapple chunks. Use your imagination and serve exotic fruits along with the more traditional.

Barbecued Prawns

Serves: 25

- 2 to 2½ lbs. (25-30 to a pound) prawns, uncooked, unpeeled, split down the back (use scissors)
- ½ c. unsalted butter
- 3 tbls. olive oil
- ¾ c. chili sauce
- 1 tbls. Worcestershire sauce
- 1 tbls. lemon juice
- 1 small lemon, sliced
- 3 cloves garlic, pressed
- 1½ tbls. minced fresh parsley
- ¾ tsp. red pepper
- ¾ tsp. paprika
- ½ tsp. dried oregano
- ¼ tsp tabasco (opt.)
- ¼ tsp. barbecue seasoning
- ¼ tsp. liquid smoke (opt.)
- Dash sugar
- Dash white pepper

Rinse and dry prawns. Spread prawns in shallow baking dish. Combine remaining ingredients in small saucepan and let simmer for 10 minutes. Pour over prawns and mix thoroughly. Cover and refrigerate 2 to 3 hours, stirring every 30 minutes. Preheat oven to 375° F and bake prawns for 15 minutes, turning once. Cook several minutes longer if necessary. **Do not** overcook. Adjust seasoning and serve with french bread. Guests peel their own prawns. Serve plenty of napkins. You may peel the prawns and prepare as above, however, do not cook as long as prawns in shells. Smaller prawns may be used to serve more guests.

To prepare in skillet: Place prawns and marinade in large skillet (cook in several batches). Cook over medium heat until prawns start to turn pink. Remove prawns and place on serving platter. Reduce liquid in skillet. Pour sauce over prawns and serve.

Macadamia Prawns

Yields: 50

- 50 large prawns, deveined and dried on paper towel
- 1 c. butter
- 2 cloves garlic, pressed
- 1½ c. finely chopped Macadamia nuts
- Lemon juice
- White pepper

Melt ¾ c. butter and let cool slightly. Dip each prawn in butter and then in chopped nuts. Melt remaining butter in large skillet and add garlic. Saute prawns on both sides until lightly pink. Season with lemon juice and white pepper. Serve immediately.

Baked Salmon
Serves: 25

- 8 to 10 lb. whole salmon
- ¼ c. lemon juice
- ¼ tsp. salt
- 6 slices bread (use day old)
- 2 tbls. butter
- 18-inch heavy aluminum foil, cut 6-inches longer than fish
- 1 small onion, sliced
- 1 small green pepper, sliced
- 1 small tomato, sliced
- ¼ tsp. thyme
- ¼ tsp. dill weed
- ½ tsp. basil leaves
- 4 slices bacon
- 4 large lemons, sliced (garnish)

Wash and dry salmon. Brush the entire fish, including the cavity, with lemon juice and sprinkle with salt. Place bread slices on aluminum foil and lay fish on top of the bread.

In a medium frying pan melt butter and add the onion, pepper, tomato, thyme, dill and basil. Stir until well mixed together. Sauté for several minutes. Fill the cavity of the fish with vegetable mixture. Place bacon across the top of fish and carefully wrap with foil. Shape the foil around fish and fold ends creating a tight seal. Place wrapped fish on a large cookie sheet. Bake in 450° F. oven for one hour.

Remove fish from oven and let rest for 10 minutes. Open foil and carefully lift fish from slices of bread and place on serving platter. It may take several people to lift fish in one piece. Discard the bread and bacon. Remove skin from fish and garnish with lemon slices. Bearnaise sauce makes a nice combination with salmon.

Salmon Spread
Yields: 2c.

- 1 can red salmon or smoked salmon, drained and bones removed (16 oz.)
- 6 to 8 oz. cream cheese
- ¼ c. green onion, chopped
- 1½ tbls. parsley, chopped
- 2 tbls. sour cream
- ⅛ tsp. white pepper
- ¼ tsp. celery salt
- ¼ tsp. liquid smoke
- Dash thyme & coriander
- Chopped parsley
- Chopped walnuts

Mix all but last two ingredients in mixing bowl. Form into two balls or logs. Roll each in walnuts and/or parsley until coated. Wrap in plastic and refrigerate for several hours until chilled. Serve with crackers. You can freeze this mixture; however, it isn't as good as freshly made. You can use pink salmon.

Chicken Liver Pâté (spread)   Yields: 3½-4 c.

3 tbls. butter
2 small white onions, chopped
1½ lbs. chicken livers
¼ lb. fresh mushrooms, chopped
½ lb. bacon, cooked, drained and crumbled
¾ c. butter
4 ozs. cream cheese
2 tbls. brandy
1 tbls. sherry
1 clove garlic, pressed

1 tsp. rosemary, crumbled
1 tsp. thyme, crumbled
½ tsp. basil, crumbled
½ tsp. nutmeg
¼ tsp. white pepper
Salt to taste
Condiments: Small sweet pickles, mustard, port wine sauce, cumberland sauce, onions
French bread or crackers

Melt 3 tablespoons butter in large skillet. Add onions, livers and mushrooms. Cook until livers are browned on the outside. Add remaining butter and let melt. Remove from heat and mix in cream cheese, brandy, sherry, garlic, rosemary, thyme, basil, nutmeg, white pepper and salt. Mix thoroughly and add bacon. Place ½ of this mixture in the blender and puree until smooth. Repeat with the second half of mixture. Place pâté in serving bowl and cover. Refrigerate for several hours or overnight. Before serving adjust seasoning if needed. Serve with thin crackers or thin slices of bread and include any or all of the condiments above.

Rumaki   Yields: 20-28

¾ to 1 lb. chicken livers
1 small can waterchestnuts, whole, drained
1 lb. sliced bacon, (10-14 slices)
Round uncolored toothpicks
2 tbls. brown sugar
1 to 2 cloves garlic, pressed

½ c. soy sauce
¼ c. white wine
¼ c. water
1 tbls. honey
¼ tsp. ground ginger
¼ tsp. 5 spice powder

Cut bacon strips in half. Lay pieces of bacon on flat work surface, place one waterchestnut in center of bacon, place one piece of liver on top of waterchestnut. Wrap bacon ends around chestnut and liver, secure with toothpick.

Mix all ingredients for marinade in shallow dish. Place the rolled rumaki in the marinade and marinate for at least one hour. You may freeze the uncooked rumaki or freeze them after baking. When ready to cook, place rumaki on a broiling pan, toothpick sideways. Broil one side, turn and broil the other side until crispy, not burnt. Serve warm. To crisp up thawed cooked rumaki, place on a cookie sheet or broiling pan and broil for several minutes on each side. You may want to substitute the following for the chicken liver: chicken meat, apple, pineapple or vegetables.

Chicken w/Bearnaise Sauce   Serves: 10-15

6 boneless, skinless chicken
   breasts cut into pieces
1 tsp. brandy or sherry

Salt and white pepper
Butter
Bearnaise Sauce

Sauté chicken in butter until lightly browned. Sprinkle with brandy or sherry. Season with salt and white pepper. Top with Bearnaise sauce and serve in a chafing dish.

Bearnaise Sauce

1 clove garlic, pressed
1 can (10¼ ozs.) Campbells Cream of
   Chicken soup
¼ c. butter
2 to 3 tsp. lemon juice

2 to 3 tsp. vinegar
½ to ¾ tsp. tarragon leaves
¼ c. finely chopped fresh parsley
2 tbls. drained capers
Salt and white pepper to taste

Sauce: Combine all ingredients in saucepan and heat until hot. Do not boil. Use over chicken, vegetables, beef or veal. May be made in advance and refrigerated for several days. Do not freeze.

Omit capers in sauce and use over meatballs for a savory flavor.

For an entreé serving, allow one to one and a half chicken breasts per person. Bearnaise sauce recipe may be doubled or tripled. You may want to cook the chicken in advance and store in large plastic bags in the refrigerator until ready to use.

Chicken Wings w/Mustard   Serves: 10-12

20 chicken wings (tips removed,
   remaining piece cut in half)
⅔ c. butter

¼ c. Dijon mustard
1¼ c. seasoned bread crumbs
¼ c. Parmesan cheese (opt.)

Melt butter and stir in mustard until well blended. Place bread crumbs in flat dish. Roll each piece of chicken in butter mixture then coat with bread crumbs. Arrange on a rack in a roasting pan or on a cookie sheet. Sprinkle with Parmesan cheese if desired. Bake in a 400 F. oven for 15 minutes. Turn and bake 15 minutes longer or until crispy.

Crispy Chicken Wings

Serves: 20-25

6 lbs. chicken wings
1 c. white wine
⅔ c. corn oil
2 (.07 oz.) packages Good Seasons Garlic Salad Dressing Mix
Parmesan cheese (opt.)

Cut off tips of wings, discard or save for making soups. Cut remaining part of wing in half. Combine wine, oil and dressing mix in a large bowl. Add wings and marinate for several hours. Turn wings once during this time. When ready to bake, place in large baking dish. Bake in 325 F. oven for 20 minutes, turning once and brushing with marinade, and bake for 20 minutes longer. For crispness, broil for several minutes on each side. Sprinkle with Parmesan cheese before broiling for added flavor. Wings may be prepared to broiling point and frozen for several weeks. Thaw and broil as above.

Chicken & Pork Pâté

Serves: 25

1 whole uncooked chicken breast
2 uncooked chicken thighs
½ c. dry white wine
½ tsp. salt
¼ tsp. white pepper
½ tsp. dried thyme leaves
2 whole cloves
12 ozs. pork sausage
1 egg, slightly beaten
1 garlic clove, pressed
⅛ tsp. allspice
6 slices bacon
French bread slices and condiments

Remove skin and bones from chicken breast and thighs. Cut chicken meat into small cubes. In a medium bowl, combine chicken cubes, wine, salt, pepper, thyme and cloves. Marinate in refrigerator 6 hours or overnight. Drain; reserve marinade. Remove and discard whole cloves. In medium bowl, combine ¼ c. reserved marinade, sausage, egg, garlic and allspice; set aside. Preheat oven to 350 F. Line a 1½ quart baking dish with bacon, letting ends extend over side. Arrange drained marinated chicken over bacon. Spoon sausage mixture over chicken. Press with the back of a spoon to pack. Pour remaining marinade over sausage mixture. Fold bacon ends over top of pâté. Cover tightly with lid or foil. Bake 1½ hours in preheated oven. Spoon off drippings. To pack pâté, top with a plate. Place a can or other heavy item on top of plate. Cool on a rack 30 minutes. Refrigerate 6 hours or overnight. Pour off drippings. Invert onto a small platter; remove dish. Remove bacon if desired. Slice and serve with French bread or crackers. Serve with mustards, port wine sauce, or small sweet pickles.

Barbecued Pork
Serves: 20-25

3½ lbs. lean pork roast or shoulder
½ c. soy sauce
¼ c. brandy
2 tbls. Grand Marnier
2 cloves garlic, pressed
¼ tsp. ground ginger
3 tbls. honey
¼ c. orange juice concentrate
½ tsp. Chinese 5 spice

Combine marinade ingredients and add pork. Marinate 12 hours. Place in shallow baking dish and bake at 300 F° for 1½ to 2 hours depending on the thickness of the pork. Baste often with the marinade. If pork is not done, cook for an additional 30 minutes. Allow meat to cool and slice thin. Serve with dipping sauce, hot mustard sauce, and sesame seeds.

Dipping Sauce
Yields: ⅔ c.

1½ tbls. orange juice concentrate
1½ tbls. catsup
1 tbls. soy sauce
1½ tbls. horseradish
1 tbls. lime juice
¼ c. dry mustard
1 slice onion
½ med. green pepper, cut
1 garlic clove, pressed

Add all ingredients together in blender, mix thoroughly.

Hot Mustard Sauce

Mix Chinese hot mustard, honey and 5 spice powder to taste.

Dolmates
Yields: 50

50 grape leaves
1 lb. ground lamb (fresh)
1½ c. cooked rice
1 medium to large onion, chopped
¼ c. chopped fresh parsley
2 c. strong beef broth

½ tsp. celery salt
¼ tsp. curry
¼ tsp. white pepper
¼ tsp. garlic powder
⅛ tsp. ground anise

Rinse leaves in hot water for several minutes. Remove small stem. Drain leaves on paper towel. In large bowl mix lamb, rice, onion and parsley. Add celery salt, curry, white pepper, garlic and anise; mix well. Lay leaves on flat work surface, vein side up. Place one to two teaspoons of filling on each leaf, depending on size of leaf. Fold sides inward, roll like a jelly roll away from you. Place in a skillet close together. Add broth and simmer for 30-40 minutes. Drain off broth and serve warm. Add lemon slices for garnish if desired. Cooked Dolmates may be frozen or refrigerated.

Dolmates are traditionally filled with either all rice or all lamb. The lamb and rice mixture above works well for catered events. An all rice mixture (with seasoning) would be less expensive for very large events. Hamburger or other meats may be substituted for the lamb.

Soups & Salads

Cream of Spinach Soup w/Cheese
Serves: 6-8

- 3 tbls. butter
- 3 tbls. oil
- 1 small onion, minced
- 20 ozs. frozen chopped spinach, thawed and drained
- 2 c. strong chicken broth
- 2 c. cream
- ½ tsp. white pepper
- Freshly grated nutmeg
- ½ lb. cooked bacon, crumbled
- 1 c. grated cheddar cheese

Melt butter and oil in large saucepan over medium heat. Add onion and cook for 5 minutes. Add spinach to onions and cook for 3 minutes, stirring frequently. Blend in broth and simmer for 10 minutes. Stir in cream, pepper and nutmeg. Continue to simmer for 5 minutes. Add bacon and cheese. Serve at once.

Oriental Soup
Serves: 8

- 1½ qts. strong chicken broth
- 6 ozs. fresh mushrooms, sliced
- 3 ozs. fresh spinach, chopped
- 1 slice fresh ginger
- 2 cloves garlic, pressed
- 2 tbls. soy sauce
- ½ tsp. sugar
- ¼ tsp. white pepper
- ⅛ tsp. ground red pepper
- ½ c. sherry
- 2 tbls. cornstarch
- 4 ozs. waterchestnuts, chopped
- 1 egg, slightly beaten
- 1 tsp. sesame oil
- ½ lb. bean sprouts
- 4 green onions, chopped

Bring broth to a boil in large pot. Reduce heat and add next 8 ingredients. Simmer for 30 minutes. Mix sherry and cornstarch together to form a thin paste. Ten minutes before serving, bring soup to a boil, stir in cornstarch mixture and continue cooking until soup is clear and slightly thickened. Stir in waterchestnuts. Remove from heat and slowly pour in egg, stirring gently with a fork until egg forms light strands. Stir in sesame oil. Divide bean sprouts and onions among soup bowls and ladle hot soup over each. Serve at once.

French Onion Soup   Serves: 8

4 to 5 tbls. butter	¼ tsp. white pepper
5 to 6 yellow onions, sliced	Salt to taste
1½ qts. strong beef broth	Dash sugar
1 c. red wine	Homemade seasoned croutons
1 c. water	Gruyere cheese, grated
2 tbls. brandy	

Melt butter in a large kettle (with lid) and stew onions slowly for 15 minutes. Do not brown. Add broth and wine, simmer for 5 minutes. Add water, brandy, pepper, salt and sugar. Place seasoned croutons in serving bowls, spoon in soup, top with cheese and serve immediately.

Leek Soup   Serves: 8-10

4½ c. strong chicken broth	2 tbls. sherry
2½ c. sliced leeks (white part)	Salt to taste
2 c. peeled, diced potatoes	White pepper to taste
1 c. cream	Chopped chives

In saucepan over high heat, combine broth, leeks and potatoes. Bring to a boil; cover, reduce heat, and simmer until vegetables are cooked. About 15 minutes. In blender mix ingredients from pan. Return to sauce pan and add cream and sherry. Season to taste. Heat through; or cover, refrigerate until needed. Sprinkle with chives before serving. May be served hot or cold.

Salad

You can buy large bags of pre-cut lettuce salads at most produce companies. Call around your area to see who sells to the public. They will be happy to tell you how many bags you will need for your function. All you have to do is rinse the lettuce and serve. Let the guests serve their dressing at the end of the serving line.

Other types of salads are available in 12 lb. to 25 lb. boxes. When buying salads wholesale, ask if there is a minimum order requirement.

Chinese Chicken Salad   Serves: 25

1 ½ to 2 lbs. bacon, fried crisp
 and drained
5 large chicken breasts, fried, cooled
 and cut into small pieces (meat only)
3 large heads lettuce, torn into
 bite-sized pieces
1 ½ c. green onions, chopped
2 (8oz.) can sliced waterchestnuts,
 drained
2 (3oz.) can chow mein noodles

Mix all ingredients except noodles in a large bowl. Chill for one hour. Add noodles and serve with dressing.

Dressing

½ c. vegetable oil
½ c. soy sauce
1 ½ tsp. dry mustard
3 tbls. honey
3 tbls. ketchup
Dash Five Spice Powder (opt.)

Mix all ingredients together in a jar or container. Chill at least one hour. Dressing is better if made the day before. Will keep a week or more in refrigerator.

Variation: Use shredded barbecued pork instead of chicken.

Almond Cheese Salad   Serves: 25

2 lbs. Gruyere cheese, shredded
10 ozs. minced ham (seasoned)
1 ½ c. slivered almonds, toasted
¾ c. chopped black olives
15 green onions, minced
Dash hot pepper sauce to taste
Fresh lemon juice
Sour cream
Salt and freshly ground pepper

Combine cheese, ham, almonds, olives, onions, pepper sauce and lemon juice in a large bowl. Add enough sour cream just to bind mixture. Season to taste. Pack into plastic or glass container and refrigerate. May be stored for up to 2 days. When ready to serve, top a lettuce leaf with large spoonful of salad mixture. Garnish with sliced almonds or other garnish suitable to salad.

Mushroom, Bleu Cheese & Walnut Salad
Serves: 6-8

¼ c. olive or salad oil
2 tsp. dry basil leaves
½ tsp. salt
⅛ tsp. each pepper & paprika
2 tsp. Dijon mustard
5 tsp. white wine vinegar
½ lb. mushrooms, sliced
2 green onions, chopped
⅔ c. broken walnut pieces
4 oz. bleu cheese, crumbled
5 c. bite-size pieces romaine lettuce
Cherry tomatoes

In a salad bowl combine, oil, basil, salt, pepper, paprika, mustard and vinegar. Beat with a fork until blended. Mix in mushrooms and green onions. Let stand at room temperature to marinate for at least 30 minutes or marinate in refrigerator for no longer than 2 hours. Add walnut pieces, bleu cheese, lettuce, cherry tomatoes and toss lightly. Chill for about 30 minutes if desired. Serve immediately.

Tomato and Pepper Salad w/Bleu Cheese Dressing
Serves: 25

10 large tomatoes, cored and sliced
5 green peppers, cored, seeded and thinly sliced into rings
Sliced fresh mushrooms (opt.)
Romaine lettuce leaves
1¼ c. cottage cheese
¾ c. milk
⅓ c. crumbled Bleu cheese
Salt & pepper to taste

Arrange tomato and pepper slices atop lettuce leaves on serving platter or individual salad plates and chill until ready to serve. Combine cottage cheese, milk and bleu cheese in blender and mix until smooth. Cover and refrigerate. When ready to serve, divide dressing among salads and top with freshly ground pepper. Serve cold.

Shrimp Salad with Mushrooms

Serves: 8

20 Large shrimp, shelled and deveined
2½ c. strong chicken broth
¼ c. sherry
16 snow peas

½ lb. fresh mushrooms, sliced
½ c. chopped macadamia nuts
3 tbls. finely minced red onion
Lettuce or spinach leaves

Dressing
2 tbls. Dijon mustard
2 tbls. lime juice
1½ tsp. dried dill-weed
6 tbls. olive oil
Salt & pepper freshly ground

Poach shrimp in gently simmering broth and sherry until pink, 2-3 minutes. Drain shrimp and let cool to room temperature, then refrigerate. Carefully slice 8 larger shrimp in half lengthwise down through tails. Reserve for garnish. Slice remaining shrimp in bitesize pieces crosswise, discarding tails. Blanch snow peas in boiling broth (from shrimp) for 2-3 minutes. Drain and dry with paper towels. Cut each pod diagonally into 3 pieces. Combine shrimp, peas, mushrooms, nuts and onion in large bowl. Add dressing to taste and toss gently. Arrange lettuce or spinach leaves on plates. Mound salad in center. Garnish each serving with 2 reserved shrimp halves. Serve with remaining dressing on the side.

Dressing
Combine mustard and lime juice in small bowl and mix well. Add chopped dill. Add oils 1 tbls. at a time whisking well after each addition. Add more lime juice if desired. Season to taste with salt and pepper.

Vegetables & Side Dishes

Bleu Cheese Onions   Serves: 6-8

3 to 4 onions, sliced
6 to 7 ozs. bleu cheese
½ c. unsalted butter

2 to 2½ tsp. Worcestershire sauce
½ tsp. dried basil or dillweed
Freshly ground white pepper

Generously butter a large baking dish. Preheat oven to 400° F. Place onions in bottom of baking dish, spreading evenly. Combine remaining ingredients in food processor just until mixed. Spread cheese mixture over onions. Bake on center rack in oven for 20 to 25 minutes. Broil briefly until top is brown and bubbly.

Green Beans w/ Waterchestnuts   Serves: 8-10

2 15 oz. cans French cut green beans, drained
8 ozs. sliced waterchestnuts, drained
2 tbls. melted butter

1 10 oz. can cream of mushroom soup
1 3 oz. can French fried onion rings
⅔ c. grated Swiss, Gruyere or Smoked Gouda cheese

Combine beans, chestnuts, butter, and soup; mix well. Lightly butter a large baking dish. Pour bean mixture into prepared dish. Top with onion rings and grated cheese. Bake in a 350° F oven for 25 to 30 minutes. Broil for several minutes until top is browned.

Gingered Carrots   Serves: 25

4-5 lbs. small French carrots,
Sherry
⅓ c. honey
½ to ¾ c. butter
1 tsp. ground ginger

⅓ c. strong orange juice (opt.)
1 to 2 tbls. Grand Marnier (opt.)
Toasted sesame seeds
Chopped fresh parsley (opt.)
Salt and white pepper

Place carrots in pan, add enough water to cover carrots. Add a large splash of sherry. Cover and cook until just starting to become tender. Do not over cook. Drain off water. Add honey, butter, ginger, orange juice and Grand Marnier. Season with salt and pepper and additional sherry to taste. To serve, sprinkle with sesame seeds and parsley. Serve hot.

Buffet Potatoes

Serves: 25

- ¼ lb. butter
- 1 c. onion, chopped
- 1 c. green pepper, chopped
- ⅓ c. flour
- 1 tsp. salt
- ½ tsp. white pepper
- 3 c. milk or ½ & ½
- 1½ lbs. Gruyere cheese, grated
- 12 c. cubed cooked potatoes
- 8 ozs. pimientos, chopped (opt.)
- 3 tbls. fresh parsley, chopped
- ⅔ c. butter, melted
- 2 to 3 c. fresh breadcrumbs
- Bacon, cooked, crumbled for garnish if desired

Preheat oven to 375° F. In large pot, melt ¼ lb. butter. Add onion and green pepper. Cook over medium heat, stirring occasionally, until tender. Blend in flour, salt and pepper (use additional seasonings if desired). Add milk, stir constantly over medium-high heat until mixture thickens. Stir in cheese and remove from heat. Place potatoes in large baking dishes. Sprinkle pimientos over potatoes and mix lightly. Divide thickened sauce among baking dishes, pouring over each dish. In a medium bowl mix breadcrumbs, parsley and ⅔ c. melted butter. Sprinkle crumb mixture over potatoes. Bake 30 to 40 minutes until heated through. Serve hot.

Tomato Timbles

Yields: 25

- 25 tomatoes, tops and pulp removed, small to medium
- 1 tbls. chopped shallots
- 3 to 4 garlic cloves, pressed
- ¼ c. flour
- ¼ c. butter
- 1 c. sherry
- 1 c. strong chicken broth
- 5 c. chopped broccoli, cooked and drained
- 1 tsp. dried basil
- Salt, white pepper and nutmeg

Drain tomato shells on a paper towel. Sprinkle shells with salt and white pepper. Set aside. In a large saucepan, cook shallots in butter for 2 minutes, blend in flour. Cook for 2 minutes more, add sherry and chicken broth. Cook until thickened and bubbly. Stir in broccoli, add basil, salt, pepper and nutmeg to taste. Remove from heat. Divide mixture between tomatoes. Place tomatoes in a baking dish just large enough to hold the tomatoes. Bake at 350° F for 20-25 minutes (depending on size). If desired, sprinkle with grated Gruyere or Parmesan cheese. Serve immediately. Do not try to reheat and serve. May be made in advance and refrigerated before baking.

Broccoli w/Bacon & Almonds

Serves: 25

5 bunches broccoli, cut off thick bottom stem and cut flowers into serving size
½ c. butter melted
¾ c. cooked crumbled bacon
½ c. sliced almonds

Cook broccoli until just tender. Place in serving dish and pour melted butter over broccoli. Top with almonds and bacon.

Rice Pilaf

Serves: 25

¾ c. butter
1 to 2 onions, chopped
4½ to 5 c. long-grained rice
6 c. strong chicken broth
Salt and white pepper to taste
Sliced almonds and/or chopped green onions

One hour before serving, melt butter in skillet over medium-high heat. Add onion and saute until transparent. Mix in rice, stirring until sizzling. Add broth and bring to boil. Reduce heat, cover and simmer for 20 minutes. Remove from heat, transfer to chafing dish and keep warm until ready to serve. May be garnished with sliced almonds and/or chopped green onions.

For Curried Rice: Add 2 tsp. curry.

For Mushroom Pilaf: Add 1½ c. sauteed fresh mushrooms.

Mushrooms w/Herbs

Serves: 8

1½ lbs. fresh button mushrooms, stems trimmed
½ c. olive oil
1 c. white wine
2 small cloves garlic, pressed
2 tbls. lemon juice
½ tsp. dried rosemary
½ tsp. dried tarragon
½ tsp. dried oregano
Pinch sugar
Salt and white pepper to taste
Fresh parsley (for garnish)

Place ingredients in saucepan. Bring to a boil and simmer for 8 minutes. Cool, chill slightly but do not let oil congeal. Serve garnished with fresh parsley.

Vegetable Casserole

Serves: 8-10

- 1½ lbs. fresh asparagus, trimmed, cooked and cut into 1-inch pieces
- 1½ lbs. fresh broccoli, cooked and cut into 1-inch pieces
- ¾ lb. fresh mushrooms, sliced and sauteed
- ¼ c. butter, melted
- ¼ tsp. nutmeg
- Salt and white pepper to taste
- ¾ c. Gruyere cheese, grated
- 1 c. Proscuitto ham, chopped
- 5 eggs, beaten
- ⅓ to ½ c. Parmesan cheese, finely grated

Place asparagus, broccoli, and mushrooms in a large buttered baking dish. Pour melted butter over vegetables. Season with nutmeg, salt, and pepper. Sprinkle with Gruyere cheese and Proscuitto ham. Cover with beaten eggs. Top with Parmesan cheese and bake at 350° F for 30 minutes or until eggs are set and top is golden brown.

Main Dishes

Lamb w/Rosemary Stuffing and Mustard Sauce
Serves: 10

1 to 1½ c. fresh bread crumbs
2 tbls. milk
3 tbls. shallots, minced
2 tbls. butter
1½ c. ground lamb

2 cloves garlic, pressed
½ tsp. crushed rosemary
½ tsp. white pepper
¼ tsp. salt
One leg of lamb, butterflied

Mustard Sauce

3 to 4 cloves garlic, pressed
½ tsp. rosemary
1½ tsp. soy sauce

½ c. Dijon mustard
4 to 5 tbls. olive oil

Make paste from bread crumbs and milk. Sauté shallots in butter. Combine paste, shallots, ground lamb, garlic, rosemary, salt and pepper. Open out butterflied leg of lamb and spread mixture over, then roll and tie roast securely. Place roast on rack in roasting pan and coat with herb and mustard sauce. Insert meat thermometer in thickest part of roast and bake at 325-350° F until desired doneness.

For Mustard Sauce: Combine garlic, rosemary, soy sauce, and mustard with a wire whip. Beat in oil by droplets to make a very thick sauce.

Glazed Ham & Sausage
Serves: 25-30

½ c. butter
4 apples cored & sliced
2 tsp. cinnamon
½ tsp. allspice
½ tsp. ground nutmeg
2½ tbls. cornstarch

3 c. apple juice
25 small, thick slices ham
25 sausage patties, cooked, drained
25 link sausage, cooked, drained
2 lbs. smoked sausage, cooked and
    cut into chunks

In large skillet, melt butter and add apple slices. Sprinkle with cinnamon, allspice and nutmeg. Cook over medium heat until apple slices are tender. Remove apples and leave juices in skillet. Blend cornstarch into juices, add apple juice. Stir constantly over medium to medium-high heat until mixture thickens. In large oven-proof dish, arrange ham, sausages and apple slices. Pour apple juice glaze over meats and apple slices. Cover and heat thoroughly. Serve hot.

Beef Burgundy
Serves: 20-25

¾ c. butter
6-6½ lbs. boneless stew meat, cut
    into 1 inch cubes
1-1¼ lbs. small white pearl onions, found in
    freezer section of most grocery stores
1 lb. fresh mushrooms, whole
    small or sliced large
⅔ c. flour
1 tbls. beef stock base
¼ c. tomato paste

4½ c. Burgundy wine
1½ c. dry Sherry
1½ c. Ruby Port
¼ c. Brandy
4 c. Beef Bouillon, undiluted
½ tsp. white pepper
3-4 cloves garlic, pressed
3 bay leaves, whole
1 lb. cooked bacon, drained (opt.)
¾ lb. peeled small French carrots (opt.)

Melt ½ the butter and brown beef cubes. Remove beef from pan and reserve. Add remaining butter to pan and add onions; cook over low heat until lightly browned. Add mushrooms and cook for 3 minutes. Remove from heat and add flour, beef stock base and tomato paste. Stir until well blended. Stir in wines, brandy and beef bouillon. Bring wine mixture to a boil, stirring, remove from heat and add beef, pepper and bay leaf. Place mixture in baking dishes and bake in a 350° F oven, covered, for approximately 1½ to 2 hours. You may take cover off for the last 45 minutes for a thicker sauce. If using bacon and carrots, mix in just before baking. Serve hot over rice or noodles. Garnish with chopped parsley or sour cream.

Epicurean Chicken Livers
Serves: 25

4½ lbs. frying chicken livers
Flour for dusting
1 c. butter
4 cloves garlic, pressed
Salt to taste
¼ tsp. white pepper

1½ lbs. sliced fresh mushrooms,
    lightly sauteed in butter
½ c. sherry
½ c. strong chicken broth
½ c. green onions, chopped
¼ c. fresh parsley, chopped
Sour cream for garnish

Rinse, drain and dry livers on paper towel. Lightly dust livers with flour. Melt ¼ of butter in a large frying pan. Add ¼ of the livers and brown quickly so they stay pink in the center. Repeat with remaining butter and livers. In a very large pan or pot add livers and remaining ingredients except sour cream, heat over medium heat until slightly thickened. Place in serving dish and top with sour cream and additional green onions or other garnish. Serve hot.

Chicken & Crab Kiev

Yields: 25

25 large, boned, Chicken breasts pounded thin
¾ lb. butter
1 to 1¼ lbs. Crab meat
Flour
Breadcrumbs (plain or seasoned)
4-6 eggs
Light cream
Fresh chopped parsley
Garlic salt and/or Celery salt
White pepper
Oil for deep frying
Gruyere cheese sauce

Mix butter, and parsley to make paste. Lay chicken breast flat, place about 2 tsp. of butter paste on chicken and spread slightly. Place small amount of crab meat in center and fold chicken encasing mixture entirely. Refrigerate until ready to fry. Prepare bowl of flour, (you may wish to season flour if using plain bread crumbs), bowl of breadcrumbs and a bowl of egg and cream mixture. Heat oil in deep fryer to 375° F. Remove chicken from refrigerator. One at a time, roll each breast in flour then egg and cream mixture, then in breadcrumbs. Place in hot oil and deep fry for 10-12 minutes until deep brown and crispy. Drain and serve with Gruyere cheese sauce. To make Chicken Cordon Bleu, substitute grated Swiss cheese and sliced Proscuitto ham for crab. Serve with the same Gruyere cheese sauce. This recipe may be used as an entrée for a luncheon or dinner style.

Gruyere Cheese Sauce

4 tbls. flour
4 tbls. butter
3 c. ½ & ½
1½ c. Gruyere cheese, grated
Milk for thinning
Salt to taste
White pepper to taste

Melt butter in saucepan and add flour to make roux. Add ½ & ½ and thin with milk to desired thickness. Add cheese and stir until melted and season to taste with salt and pepper. Serve hot.

Barbecued Spareribs

Serves: 25

15 lbs. spareribs, cut
3 celery stalks
3 large carrots

2 large onions, cut into pieces
2 c. red wine
Water

Marinade

4 c. chicken stock
2 c. soy sauce
1½ c. catsup
1 c. Sherry
1 c. pineapple juice
1 c. honey

¼ c. brown sugar
1 tsp. minced ginger
1 tsp. garlic, pressed
1 tsp. ground pepper
1 tsp. liquid smoke
Dash 5 spice powder

Glaze

1⅓ c. honey
4 tbls. soy sauce

1 tsp. ginger
¼ tsp. white pepper

Fill one or two large stockpots ½ full of water. Place ribs in each pot. Add celery, carrots, onions, and wine to pot. Bring to a boil, reduce heat and simmer until ribs are tender, about 1 hour. Drain ribs well and let cool.

For marinade: combine all ingredients and pour into shallow roasting pans. Add ribs and marinate in refrigerator for 24 hours, turning occasionally. Preheat oven to 375° F. Remove ribs from marinade and arrange on baking sheet, reserving ¾ c. marinade.

For glaze: combine all ingredients in small bowl. Stir in reserved marinade. Brush ribs generously with glaze every 10 minutes, until edges are crispy, about 20-25 minutes. Ribs may be finished on a charcoal grill rather than in the oven.

Baked Clams w/ Wine

Serves: 6

5 to 6 lbs. Butter clams, scrubbed
¼ c. butter or margarine
3 tbls. chopped fresh parsley
2 cloves garlic, pressed

2½-3 c. Chicken broth
1-1½ c. dry white wine
3 c. cooked rice
Garnish: Fresh chopped parsley
Chopped green onions

Melt butter or margarine in a medium roasting pan over medium heat. Add parsley and garlic and saute for 2 min. Pour chicken broth and wine into pan. Bring just to boil. Add clams, cover and bake in 425° F oven for 10 to 15 minutes or until clams are opened.

Spoon some hot rice into wide shallow bowl. Arrange clams on top of rice and pour broth over clams. Garnish with fresh chopped parsley or chopped green onions.

Spinach Lasagne
Serves: 20-25

Sauce

½ c. butter
½ c. flour
⅓ c. fresh basil, chopped
　or 2 tbls. dried basil
1½ tsp. fresh thyme or
　¼ tsp. dried
½ tsp. dried oregano
4 c. cream

2½ c. tomato puree
6 egg yolks
¾ tsp. salt
¾ tsp. white pepper
Nutmeg to taste
2 tbls. butter, room temp.

Lasagne

½ c. butter
3-4 medium onions, chopped
6 cloves garlic, pressed
5 to 6 lbs. fresh spinach,
　cooked, squeezed dry and chopped,
　or use 8 to 9, 10 oz. packages frozen
　spinach, squeezed dry and chopped
Salt & white pepper
Nutmeg
2 lbs. ricotta cheese, drained
1½ lbs. spicy Italian salami, minced **or**
2 lbs. crumbled cooked bacon
8 to 10 green onions, chopped

2 egg yolks
⅓ c. fresh parsley, chopped
⅓ c. fresh basil, chopped or
　2 tbls. dried
1 lb. Mozzarella cheese, grated
1 lb. Parmesan cheese, grated
6 ozs. Swiss or Gruyere cheese, grated

2 to 2½ lbs. lasagne noodles, cooked
　al dente, rinsed and drained
Additional Parmesan cheese (opt.)

For Sauce: Melt ½ c. butter in saucepan over medium heat until bubbly. Remove from heat and whisk in flour, basil, thyme and oregano. Cook, stirring constantly, about 3 to 5 minutes. Do not let flour brown. Gradually whisk in milk or cream. Increase heat slightly and cook, stirring constantly, until sauce has thickened. Stir in tomato puree. Remove from heat and let cool about 5 minutes. Whisk in egg yolks. Season with salt, pepper and nutmeg to taste. Transfer to storage containers. Spread butter over sauce to prevent skin from forming. Cover and refrigerate until ready to use.

For Lasange: Melt butter in large skillet over medium heat. Add onion and cook, stirring frequently, until browned about 25 minutes. Stir in garlic and cook for one minute. Mix in spinach and cook, stirring frequently, until dry. Remove from heat and season with salt, pepper and nutmeg to taste. Set aside and let cool. Combine ricotta, salami, green onion, egg yolks, parsley, basil in medium bowl. Mix Mozzarella, Parmesan and Swiss or Gruyere cheeses in another medium bowl; reserve 2½ c. for topping. Preheat oven to 375° F. Generously butter 2 extra large baking dishes (you may need three). Whisk through chilled sauce and adjust seasoning if needed. Spread thin layer of sauce over bottom of prepared dishes. Cover with layer of pasta. Top with thin layer of spinach mixture. Dot with ricotta mixture and sprinkle with Mozzarella mixture. Repeat layering, ending with pasta. Pour sauce over lasagne and sprinkle with reserved cheeses. Bake until bubbly and lightly browned, about 45 minutes, depending on individual ovens. Turn off heat; let lasagne stand in oven 20 minutes before cutting into squares and serving. The lasagne can be assembled without the sauce and refrigerated up to three days or frozen up to two months. Pour sauce over top before baking. The sauce can be prepared three days ahead and refrigerated. Try shredded cooked chicken instead of salami.

Spaghetti Sauce

Yields: 10 gallons

15 to 20 lbs. hamburger, fairly lean, browned and drained
10 to 11 c. onions, chopped, cooked
6 c. green pepper, chopped, cooked
5-6 c. celery, chopped, cooked
3 to 4 lbs. fresh mushrooms, sliced, lightly sauteed
3 c. fresh parsley, finely chopped or cut
25 cloves garlic, pressed

2½ to 3 gals. tomato sauce
2½ to 3 gals. chopped or stewed tomatoes
1 gal. tomato pureé
½ to ¾ gal. tomato paste
2 qts. red wine
1½ to 2 lbs. sugar
½ c. Italian seasoning
Add more Basil, Oregano, Rosemary, Thyme and Garlic as needed
Water and extra wine for thinning
40-50 lbs. spaghetti pasta, cooked
Parmesan Cheese

Divide all ingredients (except pasta and cheese) among 2 or 3 large pots. You can cook the hamburger and vegetables in the same large pots if need be, however, drain the hamburger fat and discard. Save the vegetable liquid for thinning if necessary. Allow the sauce to simmer for 2 hours. Adjust the seasoning if necessary. It is best to make the sauce several days in advance and allow the flavors to blend. You should not store tomato sauce in aluminum pots or pans. Use large, stainless steel pans to store sauce. Cover and refrigerate for several days. Several hours before serving, reheat sauce and adjust seasoning. One to one and a half hours before serving, have 2 or 3 very large pots of water starting to boil. You will need a cup of vegetable or olive oil for each pot. This will prevent the pasta from sticking together. Start cooking pasta as soon as possible. Do not try to cook pasta as you serve, you will get behind and hold up serving. Once the first pot of pasta is cooked, drain, rinse and place pasta in large, deep steamer pan. Place just enough sauce over pasta to coat lightly. You will serve the additional sauce in a serving line. This keeps the pasta from becoming dry and sticky. Cover and place prepared pans in warming oven. When ready to serve, take pans out of oven as needed. Place sauce in similar pans. Place serving of pasta on plate and top with ¼ to ⅓ c. of sauce. An ice cream scoop works well because it holds just about ⅓ c. Sprinkle with Parmesan cheese or allow the guest to serve themselves using cheese shakers. This recipe could serve 300 guests.

Cheese & Egg Scramble
Serves: 25

⅓ c. butter	1 lb. fresh mushrooms, sliced and
⅓ c. flour	lightly sauteed
3 c. milk	⅔ c. green onions, chopped
1 lb. smoked Gouda cheese, grated	¼ c. fresh parsley, chopped
1 lb. bacon	2 tbls. oil
6 slices French bread cut into ½ inch cubes	Chopped tomatoes, avocado or green onions
2½ dozen eggs	for garnish if desired

In large saucepan, melt ⅓ c. butter, blend in flour and add milk. Stir constantly over medium-high heat until mixture is thickened. Remove from heat, add cheese and stir until melted. Set aside. In a large skillet, cook bacon until crisp. Drain on paper towel, crumble and place in refrigerator. Reserve bacon drippings in skillet. Cook bread cubes in bacon drippings until crisp. Remove and set aside. Lightly butter two large oven-proof dishes. In large bowl mix eggs, mushrooms and parsley. In large skillet heat 1 tbls. oil, and ½ of the egg mixture and cook over medium heat, gently stir eggs until lightly set. Fold in ½ of the cheese mixture and turn out into oven-proof dish. Repeat with remaining ½ of egg mixture. Cover and refrigerate overnight. Just before serving, preheat oven to 350° F. Remove cover and bake eggs for 15 minutes. Top with croutons and crumbled bacon. Bake for 5 minutes longer. Garnish with chopped tomatoes, avocado or green onions if desired. Serve hot.

Easy French Toast
Yields: 25-30

10 eggs	1 tsp. cinnamon
3 c. milk	Dash allspice or nutmeg
¼ c. sugar	25-30 thick slices French
1 tbls. vanilla	Bread, day-old

In a large bowl, beat eggs, milk, sugar, vanilla, and spices until well blended. Place bread on a rimmed baking sheet. Pour egg mixture over bread and let stand for several minutes. Turn slices over and let stand until all the mixture is absorbed. Freeze, uncovered, until firm; then package airtight and return to freezer. To serve, place slices of frozen bread on lightly greased cookie sheet. Brush each slice with melted butter. Bake in a 475° F to 500° F oven for 6-8 minutes. Turn bread, brush with melted butter; bake an additional 8-10 minutes or until browned. Serve hot.

Variation: Add 2 c. crushed pineapple to the batter mixture and dip bread instead of letting it be absorbed. Cook in a lightly buttered skillet until browned on both sides. Keep cooked bread in warming oven and repeat with remaining bread. Dust with powdered sugar. Do not freeze these pieces of French toast.

Try other flavorings with French toast recipes. Serve condiments of powdered sugar, whipped butter, brown sugar, whipped cream, maple syrup, jellies and jams, or fruits.

Desserts, Punches & Misc

Macadamia Nut Fudge
Yields: Approx. 75 pieces

- 4½ c. sugar
- ½ c. unsalted butter
- 13 ozs. evaporated milk
- 12 ozs. sweet cooking chocolate
- 7 ozs. marshmellow cream
- 1 tsp. salt
- 2 tsp. vanilla
- 3 c. unsalted macadamia nuts, chopped

Combine sugar, butter, and milk in a medium saucepan and bring to a simmer over medium heat. At first sign of a bubble, simmer 5 minutes, stirring constantly. Remove from heat and add all ingredients except 1 c. nuts. Butter 2 medium-size square pans. Pour mixture into each pan and spread evenly. Sprinkle with remaining nuts, pressing lightly into surface. Chill until firm. Cut and serve in small petit four papers.

Madeleines
Yields: 25

- 1 c. butter, softened
- 2½ c. sifted powdered sugar
- 4 eggs
- 2 c. flour
- ½ tsp. vanilla
- Powdered sugar for dusting (opt.)

With an electric mixer, beat 1 c. of the butter until fluffy; gradually beat in sugar. Add eggs, one at a time, beating at high speed after each addition. Add flour and vanilla and beat until blended. Spoon 1 tbls. of the batter into each well buttered and flour-dusted madeleine cup. Bake in a 350° F oven for 20 to 25 minutes or until lightly browned. Remove from oven and immediately turn out of pan to cool. (If you only have one pan, wash, dry, and butter for next batch). Serve madeleines slightly warm or at room temperature. Or package airtight and store at room temperature for up to a week; freeze for longer storage.

French Vanilla Ice Cream w/Grand Marnier

Top French vanilla Ice Cream with 1 tbls. Grand Marnier Liqueur. Scoops of ice cream may be frozen on a cookie sheet and when ready to serve just place in dishes and top with liqueur. Serve at once.

Cake

Banana Nut Cake

10 Servings

- ⅔ c. butter, room temp.
- ⅔ c. brown sugar
- ⅔ c. granulated sugar
- 2 eggs
- 2¼ c. sifted flour
- 2¼ tsp. baking powder
- ¼ tsp. salt
- ½ c. cream
- 2 tbls. Grand Marnier
- 3 ripe bananas, mashed
- 1 c. walnuts, chopped
- Frosting, recipe below

Cream butter and sugars in mixing bowl. Add eggs one at a time, beating after each addition. Sift together dry ingredients and add to butter mixture alternately with milk and Grand Marnier beginning and ending with dry ingredients. Fold in mashed bananas and walnuts. Pour into 2 greased 9-inch round or square cake pans. Preheat oven to 350° F. Place cake pans on center rack in oven. Bake until toothpick inserted comes out clean. About 45 minutes. Let cool on wire rack for one hour.

Frosting

- 1 c. butter, room temp.
- 1 c. granulated sugar
- 3 eggs
- 2 tsp. instant coffee granulars
- ¼ c. Kahlua

Cream butter and sugar in mixing bowl. Using high speed of mixer, add eggs one at a time, beating after each addition. Blend in coffee granulars dissolved in Kahlua to better and egg mixture.

Garnishes

- 2 small ripe bananas
- 1 tbls. Kahlua
- 1 tbls. Grand Marnier
- ½ c. chopped Macadamia nuts, unsalted

To assemble cake:

Place one layer of cooled cake on serving platter. Spread a very thin layer of frosting on top of first layer. Slice 1½ bananas and cover top of frosted first layer. Sprinkle with Kahlua and spread about half of remaining frosting over bananas. Place second layer over first. Spread remaining frosting over top (only) of second layer. Slice remaining ½ banana and garnish top of frosted cake. Sprinkle chopped Macadamia nuts over cake, serve or let stand in refrigerator for up to one hour. When ready to serve, sprinkle the Grand Marnier over bananas on top of cake.

Gingerbread

2½ c. all purpose flour
1 tbls. instant coffee (not freeze-dried)
1½ tsp. cinnamon
2 tsp. ginger (ground)
½ tsp. cloves (ground)
1 tsp. baking soda
½ tsp. salt
½ c. unsalted butter, room temp.
¾ c. dark brown sugar, packed
2 eggs
1 c. molasses
1 c. buttermilk
½ tsp. freshly grated nutmeg
Applesauce (opt.)

Preheat oven to 375° F. Butter and flour a 9-inch square baking pan. Sift together flour, coffee powder, spices, baking soda and salt. Set aside.

Cream butter and brown sugar with electric mixer until light and fluffy. Add eggs one at a time, beating well after each addition. Add molasses and beat about 2 minutes, scraping bowl often. With mixer on lowest speed, add sifted dry ingredients in thirds alternately with buttermilk, beginning and ending with dry ingredients. Scrape sides of bowl frequently and do not overbeat. Turn into baking pan and bake until gingerbread tests done with toothpick, about 50-55 minutes. Serve warm or at room temperature. Top with applesauce.

Pumpkin Rum Mousse

2 tsp. gelatin
2 tbls. dark rum
2 egg yolks, beaten
3 tbls. sugar
½ c. canned pumpkin
¼ tsp. cinnamon
⅛ tsp. allspice
⅛ tsp. nutmeg
½ c. whipping cream
Additional whipped cream

Sprinkle gelatin over rum in small bowl and let stand until softened. Place bowl over simmering water and stir until gelatin completely dissolves. Beat yolks with sugar until thick and lemon colored. Fold in pumpkin and spices. Stir in gelatin-rum mixture. Spoon into individual molds or mousse cups and chill thoroughly. Garnish with additional whipped cream.

Sour Cream Breakfast Cake
Serves: 10

Cake
- 2 c. granulated sugar
- ¾ c. butter
- 2 eggs
- 1 c. sour cream
- 1 tsp. vanilla
- 2 c. flour
- ½ tsp. salt
- ¼ tsp. allspice
- 1 tsp. baking soda
- ½ c. raisins
- ¼ c. chopped nuts

Topping
- ¼ to ½ tsp. cinnamon
- ¼ c. brown sugar
- ½ c. chopped nuts

Cake: Cream together sugar, butter, and eggs. Add sour cream, vanilla, flour, salt, allspice, baking soda, raisins, and chopped nuts; mix well. Pour batter into two 8-inch or 9-inch greased pans.

Topping: Combine cinnamon, brown sugar, and chopped nuts. Sprinkle over cake mixture.

Bake at 350° F for one hour. Cover with foil for the last 15 minutes to prevent burning the topping.

Small Biscuits
Serves: 10-12

- 2 c. unbleached all purpose flour
- 2 c. cake flour (not self-rising)
- 1 tsp. salt
- 2 tbls. plus 2 tsp. baking powder
- ½ c. unsalted butter, well chilled
- 1¼ to 1½ c. chilled milk

Preheat oven to 425° F and grease a large baking sheet. Combine dry ingredients in deep bowl. Using a pastry blender, cut in butter until mixture is course and mealy. With fork, add milk and toss gently. Do not overmix; use only enough milk to make dough moist but not wet. Turn mixture onto floured board and gently knead 2 or 3 times. Roll or pat into rectangle ½-inch thick. Cut into 1-inch squares. Transfer to prepared sheet, spacing about ⅛-inch apart. Bake until puffed and golden, 10 to 15 minutes. Dough can be prepared 1 day ahead, wrapped and refrigerated overnight. If baking biscuits ahead, let cool, then slit each biscuit on three sides. Immediately transfer to airtight plastic bags and freeze. Defrost in refrigerator the day before serving. Shortly before serving, warm in 350° F oven for 6 to 8 minutes. Serve with honey and jams or sliced Prosciutto ham and mustard.

Brunch Rolls

Yields: 24 rolls

½ c. milk
½ c. water
½ c. honey
¼ c. butter
2 tbls. Grand Marnier or rum
2 tbls. dry yeast
½ c. warm water
1 tsp. honey

3 eggs, beaten
1 tsp. fresh lemon juice
1 tsp. salt
½ tsp. cinnamon or allspice
½ tsp. finely grated orange peel
7 c. unbleached flour
Orange juice

Bring milk and water to boil in small saucepan over high heat. Remove from heat and add ½ c. honey, butter and Grand Marnier. Stir until butter is melted; cool to room temperature. Combine yeast, warm water, and 1 tsp. honey in a large mixing bowl and stir until yeast is dissolved. Let stand until foamy, about 5 minutes. Add milk mixture, eggs, lemon juice, salt, cinnamon, orange peel, and 3½ c. flour. Beat in one direction for 30 seconds. Let stand until mixture bubbles, about 20 minutes. Beat in remaining flour. Turn dough out onto a lightly floured surface and knead until soft. Transfer to oiled bowl, turning to coat all surfaces. Cover and let rise in warm area until doubled in bulk, about 1 hour. Punch dough down and knead several times to remove air bubbles. Divide dough into 24 pieces. Shape into small balls and place in greased muffin pans. Brush each roll with orange juice. Cover and let rise until doubled. Preheat oven to 350° F. Bake until golden brown, about 45 minutes. Let cool 5 minutes. Turn rolls out onto rack and let cool completely.

Bran Muffin

1⅔ c. flour
1 c. sugar
6 ozs. raisin bran cereal
⅓ c. raisins (opt.)
1⅔ tsp. baking soda

⅔ tsp. salt
1⅓ c. butter
2 eggs, beaten
⅓ c. oil

Combine first six ingredients in a large bowl and mix well. Combine buttermilk, eggs and oil in another bowl. Stir buttermilk mixture into dry ingredients just until blended. Cover and refrigerate for at least 2 hours or overnight. When ready to bake, preheat oven to 400° F. Fill greased muffin tins no more than ¾ full and bake until toothpick comes clean.

Creamed Chocolate
Serves: 25

2 c. unsalted butter, softened
1½ c. sugar
16 ozs semisweet chocolate, melted
12 eggs
¼ c. brandy or orange flavored liqueur
Whipped cream for garnish

With an electric mixer or in a food processor, beat butter and sugar at high speed until well blended. Slowly pour in chocolate and continue beating until blended. Still at high speed, beat in eggs, one at a time, until thoroughly blended. If desired, mix in liqueur. Spoon into 25 small individual dishes. Cover and refrigerate for at least 4 hours or up to 3 days. Just before serving, garnish each dish with a dollop of whipped cream. Sprinkle with shaved chocolate and/or sliced almonds.

Orange Cranberry Sauce

1 to 1¼ c. sugar
½ c. fresh orange juice
½ c. water
3 c. fresh cranberries, rinsed and stemmed
2 tbls. Cognac
1 tbls. finely grated orange peel
1 tbls. fresh lemon juice

Combine sugar, orange juice and water in large saucepan and bring to boil over medium-low heat, stirring until sugar is dissolved. Add berries and cook until popped, 5 to 7 minutes. Mash some of berries with back of spoon. Remove pan from heat. Cool 5 minutes. Blend in remaining ingredients. Cool completely. Refrigerate sauce until ready to serve.

Sherbet w/Champagne
Serves: 25

25 scoops lemon, pineapple or other flavored sherbet
25 dessert cups or wine glasses
2 bottles champagne, well chilled

When ready to serve, place scoop of sherbet in each dish or glass. Pour small amount of champagne over sherbet. Serve immediately.

Garlic Bread
Serves: 300

30 (handwritten: 10) loaves French bread, cut into thick slices
2 to 2½ lbs. margarine, melted
10 (handwritten: 30) or more garlic cloves, pressed
Garlic salt to taste
Other seasoning optional *oregano*

Combine margarine and seasonings. Brush each slice and wrap loaf in foil. Cover completely. Store in refrigerator. Heat in oven 30 minutes before serving.

Easy Mulled Punch
Serves: 12-15

1 fifth burgundy wine
1 quart cranberry juice
1 quart pineapple juice
¼ to ⅔ c. brown sugar, packed
¼ tsp. cinnamon
½ tsp. cloves, ground
¼ tsp. ginger

Combine all ingredients in large pan and heat slowly, stirring occasionally. Do not boil. Ladle into mugs or heat-proof glasses.

Cappuccino
Serves: 6-8

3 c. coffee
3 c. cream
½ c. dark creme de cocoa
¼ c. rum
¼ c. brandy

Combine all ingredients and heat in saucepan. Serve immediately.

Milk Punch
Yields: 1 quart

2 c. vanilla ice cream
1 c. milk
½ c. bourbon
¼ c. light rum
3 tbls. brandy
Grount nutmeg

Stir ice cream to soften. Mix in remaining ingredients. Serve in punch cups with a dash of nutmeg on top.

### Waikiki Punch	Yields: 6 qts.

1½ qts. pineapple juice
2 qts. orange juice
2 c. coke
1 pint dark rum
1 pint light rum
1 qts. gingerale
Fresh pineapple (garnish)
Ice

Combine all ingredients in large punch bowl. Serve in punch cups with pineapple garnish.

### Champagne Punch	Serves: 25

2 quarts 7-up
2 quarts gingerale
2 quarts orange juice
2 quarts champagne
Large chunks of ice
Sherbet ice cream

Mix 7-up, gingerale, orange juice and champagne in large punch bowl. Add ice and stir until well blended. Add scoops of sherbet. Serve as soon as possible.

Pineapple or lemon sherbet seem to taste the best. Colors like lime green tend to give the punch a dirty color.

### Chocolate Eggnog	Serves: 10

7 c. milk
¾ c. chocolate syrup
4 egg yolks
½ c. creamy peanut butter (opt.)
2 tsp. vanilla
4 egg whites
1 c. whipping cream, whipped
Ground cinnamon

Process 3½ c. milk, chocolate, egg yolks, peanut butter, and vanilla in a blender until foamy; pour into punch bowl. Stir in remaining milk. Beat egg whites until stiff peaks form and fold into milk mixture. Fold in whipped cream. Sprinkle lightly with cinnamon. Serve in punch cups.

Spices

Chinese Five-Spice Powder

2 tbls. cracked black peppercorns
12 3-inch sticks whole cinnamon
12 whole star anise
30 whole cloves
2 tbls. fennel seeds

Pulverize all ingredients to a powder in a blender, electric grinder or mortar. Stores for one year. Use sparingly with meat and poultry; never more than ½ tsp. per lb. of meat.

Curry Powders

Mild

1 tbls. whole black peppercorns
1 tbls. whole cumin seeds
1 3-inch stick whole cinnamon
½ tbls. coriander seeds
4 whole cloves
1 tsp. cardamom seeds (extracted from pods)
2 tsp turmeric
¾ tsp. seeds from dried chili-pepper pods

Pulverize all ingredients in a blender, electric grinder or mortar. If necessary put through sieve to achieve a fine powder after pulverizing.

Hot

1½ tsp. whole cumin seeds
1 tsp. coriander seeds
1 tsp. whole black peppercorns
1 tsp. turmeric
1 tsp. dried chili peppers
¾ tsp. ground ginger
½ tsp. cayenne pepper

Blend all ingredients together and store in screw top jar.

Note: You may improvise on these curry powder recipes by choosing from the following list of spices. Not all, of course, should be used in any one blend, but black pepper is a must, and coriander, cumin, and turmeric are basics. Add a small amount for starters until you find your perfect blend.

Black whole peppercorns
Dried chili peppers
Whole cloves
Cinnamon sticks
Cardamom seeds
Whole coriander seeds
Whole cumin seeds
Ginger
Whole mace (blades)
Ground nutmeg
Whole allspice
Turmeric
Mustard seed
Poppy seed
Anise
Bay leaves

Hints For The Healthy

Catered foods usually tend to be high in calories. Special occasions allow us the pleasure of indulging in foods we don't normally eat. By no means should anyone consume large quantities of salt, fat, sugar, etc.

Some recipes in this book are definately not for dieters. However, I have listed ways in which you can adapt recipes to fit your particular needs. These suggestions will make the items on your menu more nutricious and beneficial.

1. Use low calorie and/or sodium cheeses.
2. Lowfat cottage cheese mixed with a small amount of buttermilk or lemon juice makes a sour cream substitute.
3. When possible use honey instead of sugar.
4. Offer a low calorie/fat/salt salad dressing in addition to regular styles of dressings.
5. Season with herbs and spices instead of salt.
6. Use fresh foods instead of canned or frozen.
7. Remove skin and fat from poultry, fish and meats.
8. Serve fresh fruit and vegetable trays.
9. Use fresh vegetable and/or fruit slices for canapés instead of breads and crackers.
10. Cut down on smoked foods, as they are high in salt.
11. Broil foods instead of frying.
12. Serve non-alcoholic wines or low calorie beers.
13. Read labels carefully.
14. Check local health food stores for additional information.

Freezer Storage

Meat, uncooked
Beef & Lamb
    Roasts . . . . 9-12 mo.
    Steaks & chops . . . . 9-12 mo.
    Ground . . . . 4-6 mo.
    Liver, heart, tongue . . . . . . 3-4 mo.

Pork
    Roasts . . . . 4-6 mo.
    Chops . . . . 4-6 mo.
    Ground & variety . . . . 1-3 mo.

Meat, cured & smoked
Ham & bacon . . . . 1-3 mo.
Cold cuts & sausage . . . . . . 1-2 mo.

Meat, cooked
Beef & lamb
    Roasts . . . . 4-6 mo.
    Stews & pies . . . . 2-4 mo.
Pork
    Roasts . . . . 2-4 mo.

Poultry, uncooked
Chicken & turkey . . . . 9 mo.
Duck & geese . . . . 6 mo.
Giblets . . . . 3 mo.

Poultry, cooked
Chicken & turkey . . . . 2 mo.
    In broth or gravy . . . . 6 mo.

Fish
Cod, perch, bluefish,
    haddock . . . . 9 mo.
Lake bass, flounder,
    sunfish, bluegill . . . . 7-8 mo.
Whitefish, lake trout,
    catfish, pike, shrimp . . . . . . 4-5 mo.

Dairy
Butter . . . . 6-8 mo.
Cheese
    Cottage, uncreamed . . . . 3 mo.
    Soft . . . . 3 mo.
    Hard . . . . 6-8 mo.
Margarine . . . . 1 yr.
Ice cream & sherbet . . . . 2 mo.
Eggs
    Whites, uncooked . . . . 1 yr.
    Yolks, uncooked . . . . 1 yr.

Fruits
Citrus . . . . 6 mo.
Others . . . . 1 yr.

Vegetables
Most vegetables . . . . 1 yr.

Other
Breads, baked
    Yeast . . . . 6-8 mo.
    Quick . . . . 2-4 mo.
Cakes & cookies
    Frosted . . . . 2-4 mo.
    Unfrosted . . . . 6-8 mo.
Coffee
    Ground . . . . 2 mo.
Flour . . . . 1 yr.
Nuts . . . . 1 yr.
Pie shell
    Unbaked . . . . 6-8 mo.
Sugar, brown . . . . 6-12 mo.
Sandwiches
    Some . . . . 1-3 wk.
Appetizers . . . . 1-3 mo.

Do not add cloves or garlic to dish before freezing; flavors will become stronger. Onions will lose flavor. Little change will occur with cinnamon and nutmeg. Pepper and sage may get stronger. Curry can take on a musty flavor.

Be careful when thawing certain foods; some will start to spoil very quickly. Label every package before placing in the freezer. Know what is in your freezer and don't leave items in so long they become spoiled. This is a waste of time and money.

Spread bread with cream cheese or butter before filling with spreads and freezing. This will keep the bread from gettng soggy. Freeze sandwiches in layers on a cookie sheet.

Do not freeze: Lettuce, radishes, celery, tomatoes, cucumbers, chopped egg whites, mayonnaise and gelatins.

CHAPTER 7

BEVERAGE
WINE
BAR SET-UP
BEVERAGE QUANTITIES

Do not allow your guests to consume large quantities of alcoholic beverages. You may want to consult an attorney concerning your legal responsibility for guests who drink to excess.

Offer three to five varieties of wines. Allow your guests to sample each before making their selection.

Beverage quantities will depend on the type of function. Guests will always consume more liquid in hot weather. Plan beverages in accordance with your budget in mind.

Beverage

Depending on your preceding decisions, you will need to choose the beverage and service best suited to your function. Keep in mind the time of day, type of function, budget, location, license or permit, menu and general age of guests.

If you do not wish to have alcoholic beverages, you should serve a punch or soft drink, especially in warm weather. A simple juice punch is very inexpensive to prepare for large groups.

Keg beer is less expensive than bottled beer but you might need someone to deliver and set up the kegs. You will also need some means to cool the beer. Rental companies have keg containers made of heavy plastic which keep beer cold for quite some time. A large, clean garbage can will work just as well. Place ice on top and around the sides of the keg.

Wine is less expensive if purchased in large bottles or boxes. You will have to decide on quality or quantity. A champagne punch will cut your wine cost considerably. You can purchase wine from some wholesalers at what they call "dock sales". Call the wine wholesaler first and ask if you can purchase wine without a license.

Check with local wine shops about wine tastings that may be offered in your area. Pages 78-84 will give you a great deal of information on wines.

When considering a full bar set-up, remember that this is the most expensive way to serve your guests. A rented portable bar will cost between $20.00-$40.00 depending on the size of bar needed. Bartenders will charge from $7.00 to $25.00 per hour depending on experience and duties required. If you allow the bartender to accept tips, they may reduce their fee. A friend will sometimes help out and tend bar for you, but make sure they are qualified to handle the job. When in doubt, hire or ask an extra person to help.

Mixers are the next things to consider. You will find a chart on page 85 to help you determine what is needed for your bar set-up.

Caterers will sometimes be able to supply alcoholic beverages for your function. Ask the caterer if they have the proper license to sell or supply alcoholic beverages. Most caterers will quote seperate prices for bar set-up and bartenders, but you may have to supply the liquor. Restaurants and hotels offer this service within their establishments. Prices will vary, so get all quotes in writing before you decide what type of beverage service will be best.

Use the following pages to help you learn more about wines. Plan your own wine tasting with friends and relatives. Have each person bring one bottle of wine and you supply the snacks.

Wine
Grape Names and Areas

The Europeans name their wines after areas in which the grapes are grown. On the West Coast we grow many of the same grape varieties as the Europeans and we name those resulting wines by the grape names, i.e., the varietal name, when they are primarily of one grape type. In Europe, the laws govern what grapes can be grown in what areas. These laws have taught them the optimum varietals for their soils and climates.

In the U.S., our experience has not fully determined which types should grow where, so instead of telling growers what they may plant, our laws tell them what they may call their wines, i.e., what name they may carry on their label. To the novice American wine drinker, our system seems reasonably simple and the European one tremendously complex. However, a little exposure to the basic areas of France, i.e., Burgundy, Bordeaux, Loire Valley, Rhone Valley, etc., and the American consumer soon realizes that certain tastes can be associated with place names as easily as they can be with the specific varietal names.

The same can be said for the wine producing valleys of Germany, Italy, Spain, and Portugal. A little exposure to those tastes and we soon lose our apprehension of not knowing what sort of wine we are getting.

The same grapes grown in two different parts of the world will not produce exactly the same wine. There will be family characteristics that will be common, but the difference is soil, climate, and wine making techniques will insure they are not identical. The argument may never end that determines who makes the very best of virtually any of the top varietals.

Wine Terminology

RED WINES

1. **Light** — Not having dark color nor heavy tannic property.

2. **Fruity** — Similar to saying off dry about a white. Red wines seldom have any sugar remaining but this term refers to wines whose fruit properties are predominate and make the taster think of sweetness. Gamay Beaujolais.

3. **Full bodied, heavy, tannic, powerful** — All terms to describe big red wines with full dark color and heavy tannin-filled tastes. These wines are not for most novices. With time these wines lose their tannin and become softer. Cabernet Sauvignon, Red Bordeaux, and some Zinfandels fit this description.

4. **Soft** — In reds this means easy to drink, can refer to acid level or to mature wine that has mellowed out. A key for novice enjoyability.

5. **Hard** — See 3. Can also refer to a young red wine that is rough and aggressive in the mouth.

6. **Life** — In red wines longevity depends on acid level, tannin level, and fruit intensity. The greatest wines will take years to mellow out, will have barrel characteristics, but will still maintain fruit smells and tastes.

7. **Tannin** — Part of the grape that makes your teeth feel like they are wearing sweaters amd makes you pucker. This component is necessary to help hold the wines together. Its effect can be diminished by eating food while drinking.

8. **Drinkability, Approachability** — Wines age at different speeds. The more tannin and acid a wine has, the longer it will take to become drinkable or approachable.

WHITE WINES

1. **Dry** — Opposit of sweet: Dry wines have all fruit sugar converted to alcohol by the fermentation process.

2. **Off dry or medium dry** — Wines with small amounts of unfermented sugar (residual sugar) remaining after fermentation. These **are not** sweet wines and should never be referred to as such since most people have a negative view of that word. Fruity is a common description for such wines.

3. **Crisp, clean, refreshing** — Wines with good natural acid levels are crisp. Acid adds sparkle and liveliness to wine taste just as it does to apples and fruits. Too much acid makes novices say "tart". Wines with some residual sugar can take more acid because sugar and acid "balance" each other in white wines. Wines with good acid/sugar balance leave the mouth refreshed, not dulled or heavy.

4. **Flabby** — Wine without good acid level. Tasting heavy in the mouth and lifeless. Needing zing.

5. **Soft** — Low acid wine but not quite flabby. For the novice they will seem just right. For the experienced wine drinker they will lack life but may still be acceptable.

6. **Fruity** — Tasting of the grapes themselves instead of some other part of the winemaking process. This is a complimentary term, often infers slight sweetness.

7. **Oaky** — Smelling and tasting of the fine oak barrels some of the more expensive white wines are aged in. Generally reserved for the best of the dry white types made from Sauvignon Blanc or Chardonnay grapes. Too much oak overpowers fruit character.

8. **Balance** — Normally used to describe the mix between sugar and acid in off dry wines. Sometimes it is used to decribe wines that show both fruit and oak.

9. **Novice** — Inexperienced drinker with regard to wine. Will normally prefer off dry, soft whites. As a novice drinks more he/she will normally move slowly toward drier and crisper wines.

The following pages contain information of grape varieties and wine names. It will also tell you where in the U.S. and Europe these grapes grow.

This information is designed to inform the novice wine drinker as well as the experienced wine drinker. This does not cover every aspect of wine, but it will give you quite an insight into wine in general.

Grape Variety and U.S. Name	European Growing Area and Wine Name
WHITE	
1. **Chenin Blanc**	Vouvray, Loire Valley, France.
2. **Sauvignon Blanc** (often called Fume Blanc)	Graves, Sauternes, and the other subdistricts of Bordeaux, France.
3. **Semillon**	Same areas as Sauvignon Blanc.
4. **Gewurztraminer**	Alsace, France, also some in Germany and Switzerland. In an exception to the rule, the wine will be named after the grape in Alsace.
5. **White Riesling** **Johannisberg Riesling**	Mosel and Rhine Valley of Germany. Also, Alsace, where it is just called Riesling.
6. **Sylvaner**	Rhine Valley where it is a major component of most Liebfraumilch. This and several other such grapes are somewhat like true Riesling but not as fine, as classy. They are used for lower quality, higher production wines, often good values but sometimes grossly overpriced.
7. **Monterey Riesling, Grey Riesling, Sylvaner Riesling Riesling**	These are American names for grapes that fit the general description given under Sylvaner; sometimes they produce good wines for the money; sometimes they are just trying to ride the true Riesling's good name.
8. **Pinot Noir Blanc**	This grape grows in Burgundy where it produces great red wines but is not used for white wine. In the U.S., it is a result of needing white wine to meet demand but having red grapes.
9. **Chardonnay (sometimes called Pinot Chardonnay)**	Cote D'Or, Chablis, Macon, Pouilly Fuisse, and Beaujolais, all in Burgundy. This grape produces the best dry whites of both the U.S. and Europe.
10. **Pinot Blanc**	Another Burgundy white grape, not quite as prized as Chardonnay. Little is grown in the U.S.

RED

1. **Gamay (sometimes called Napa Gamay)** — Beaujolais, Beaujolais Villages, and the more prestigious individual villages such as Morgan in the Beaujolais district in southern Burgundy.

2. **Gamay Beaujolais** — This grape's true identity has recently been discovered and it can legally be called either this name or Pinot Noir. However, it is not the finest clone of the Pinot Noir family. Makes very good light wines. Heavily grown in CA, it is not so wisdespread in Europe.

3. **Pinot Noir** — The prestigious Cote D'Or, the best Burgundy. Also grown in Italy, Switzerland, Germany and other countries. The benchmark reference is Burgundy, though CA does fairly well, and is getting better. The NW seems full of potential.

4. **Zinfandel** — The origin of this grape remains a mystery and there is presently no exact European duplicate. In the U.S., it makes a range of wines from white to red, light to heavy, fair to great.

5. **Cabernet Sauvignon** — Bordeaux, France. Many great wines are grown here. The best are bottled under Chateau or Estate labels, such as Chateau Lafite Rothschild or Ch. Mouton Rothschild. Considered by many to be the world's best red grape, it also produces great wine in CA and the NW.

6. **Merlot** — This grows in Bordeaux also, where it is blended with the Cabernet Sauvignon to improve both wines. That practice is growing in this country, though it is also bottled seperately and ranges from heavy and long-lived to medium weight and ready to consume.

7. **Malbec Petite Verdot** — Three more Bordeaux grapes with family similarities to Cabernet. Little is grown in the U.S.

8. **Petite Sirah** — Probably a seldom-planted Rhone Valley grape. There the results are disappointing but in CA it ranges from fair to great.

9. **Syrah** — The great grape of Chateauneuf Du Pupe, Hermitage and the other fine wine areas of the Rhone Valley. Very limited U.S. plantings.

10. **Barbera Grignolino** — This grape grows in Italy. There are some plantings in CA. Good wine but not as heavy as the Nebbiolo.

11. **Nebbiolo** — The great red grape of Italy where it produces Barolo, Barbaresco, Gattinara, and others. Little planted in the U.S.

ROSE

1. **Cabernet Sauvignon** — Makes excellent pink wines in CA and the NW but is seldom used for this purpose in Europe.

2. **Pinot Noir** — Same as Cabernet Sauvignon in that it is seldom used in Europe.

3. **Grenache** — Anjou, Loire Valley where it makes Rose D'Anjou. Also Tavel, Rhone Valley, and many other European area roses.

4. **Cabernet Franc** — Anjou, Loire Valley, makes Cabernet D'Anjou. Little is grown in the U.S. and seldom used for rose.

5. **Gamay/Gamay Beaujolais** — These two similar grapes are often used in the U.S. for rose but their European counterparts are seldom seen here.

6. **Vin Rose** — This is not a grape type but a generic name; not a varietal name. The wines are blended from various grapes both in the U.S. and in Europe. The well-known Portugese roses, Mateus and Lancers are good examples.

SPARKLING

1. **Pinot Noir, Pinot Blanc, Pinot Chardonnay** — These are grapes used in the true Champagne district of France. They also produce the best sparkling wines of CA.

2. **Chenin Blanc, Sauvignon Blanc** — Loire Valley, especially Vouvray and the Saumur areas.

3. **Muscat** — Town of Asti, Italy, wine is called Asti Spumanti.

4. **White Riesling** — Mosel and Rhine Valleys, Germany.

Note about Burgundy and Chablis

Burgundy is a part of France that produces highest quality wines, both red and white. In California, Burgundy is a generic name for lower end red wine, but not a grape variety.

Chablis is a city within Burgundy that produces fine white wines from the revered Chardonnay grape. In California, Chablis is a generic name for lower quality white wine, not a grape variety.

Where To Buy Wines

Most larger cities will have a variety of wine shops. Some of these stores or businesses will hold small wine tastings, giving you a chance to taste several wines available in their stores. Call a local wine shop or check your newspaper for tastings in your area.

Many delicatessens will also carry wines and beers. They will help you choose wines for your menu. Almost any city has specialty shops; check your phone book for locations near you.

Check with bookstores for wine books or guides. You can learn a great deal about wines by just looking through these books. Your local library is also a good source of information about wines.

If you are interested in learning more about wines, ask a wine shop about classes they may offer. Some Community Colleges offer special classes to the public.

Have fun with wines and try different varieties. Visit a local winery or take a bus tour through your area wineries. You may find information on tours in the newspaper or by asking your wine shops.

How Much Beverage

How much coffee or punch
One gallon of punch will serve approximately 25 people.

One pound of coffee will serve about 75 people, depending on the size of cups used. Fresh ground coffee will yield stronger coffee than canned.

How much champagne
One case of champagne (12 fifths) will serve 50-60 people. This will give you from 80 to 90 drinks.

How much liquor
A non-professional bartender will pour approximately 16 to 18 drinks per fifth of liquor.

A professional bartender will pour approximately 20-22 drinks per fifth of liquor.

Bar set-up for 50-60 people

Liquor:
- 4 fifths Vodka
- 2 fifths Scotch
- 2 fifths Gin
- 2 fifths Bourbon
- 1 pint Vermouth
- ½ case white wine
- 1 case beer

Mixer:
- 4 qts. tonic
- 4 qts. soda
- 5 qts. 7-up
- 2 qts. cola
- 2 qts. diet cola
- 3 qts. orange juice
- 2 qts. ginger ale
- 2 qts. collins mix
- 1 qt. tomato juice
- 3-4 qts. water

Supplies:
- 1 small jar olives
- 1 small jar cherries
- 1 small jar onions
- 3-4 lemons
- 6 limes
- tabasco and/or bitters
- plastic picks
- sugar cubes
- cloth & paper towels
- 125-150 cocktail napkins
- 40-45 lbs. cocktail ice
- 1 portable bar
- 1 bartender

The amount of liquor and mixers will depend on how long the party will last and how much you want to allow your guests to consume.

Many states have very strict laws. Play it safe and don't let your guests drink too much.

CHAPTER 8

INVITATIONS
DECORATIONS
RENTAL ITEMS
STAFF

Be creative and design your own invitations. Allow at least two weeks for mailed invitations to reach your guests. Weddings and reunions may require mailings a month or more in advance.

Remember not to overdo the decorations. An empty facility appears to need a great deal of decoration. However, when guests arrive the open spaces will balance out.

Quality of rental items will vary from one company to another. Always visit a display room before choosing a rental company.

The number of staff members needed for an event will depend on the type of menu and set-up used. If guests will be serving themselves, you may need fewer staff servers. When in doubt, have an extra helper.

Invitations

Invitations are usually fairly expensive if you are having them printed, placed in envelopes, and mailed. If you watch sales you can find packages of invitations for as much as 50% off the regular price. Pre-printed invitations are available at many party supply stores. Lines are provided for you to write in the information needed for your function.

One suggestion is to have a large rubber stamp made and buy blank invitation size cards at a stationary store. Printing your own cards can save much time and money. You will be able to find all colors and shapes of cards at most stores.

If you are artistic you could design and photocopy or print your own invitations. Whatever type of invitation you choose, be sure to allow plenty of advance notice for your guests. You may want to have your guests call and let you know if they are coming to your function. Putting R.S.V.P. on your invitations informs the guests that they are required to respond as soon as possible.

Since postage is a major expense these days, you might consider hand delivery or phone invitations. This procedure is less formal and is acceptable for many types of functions. Divide the guest list among friends who want to help. This will save considerable time.

The invitation styles will vary depending on the types of events given. Do not feel that you must spend a great deal of time and money on your invitations. As long as the guests are informed, that is all that matters.

Decorations

Decorations will vary depending on your individual function. Many times the simplest can be the nicest. Many book stores carry books and guides on how to decorate using household items. This can save you a great deal of money if your budget is limited.

Outdoor flowers are free, so ask your friends and neighbors if you can use some flowers from their gardens for your event. By utilizing household plants, you can make groups of plants and flowers on the food table, or in spaces around the room.

Wholesale florist's supply companies usually do not allow the public to purchase cut flowers or plants without a nurserymans' license. You may find some smaller companies that will sell to the public. Check your telephone book and call several businesses in your area to get further information. If you can purchase plants and flowers from such businesses, the savings will be considerable.

Community Colleges sometimes offer short term flower arranging classes or you can buy arranging books from a florist supply store or gardening center.

The following page will give some ideas for decorating and serving. When you see a clever or interesting decorating or serving technique write it down for future use.

Decorating and Serving Suggestions

Use a large wood or plastic cutting board covered with leafy lettuce for a handy serving platter for cheese and/or meats.

Pizza cardboard rounds covered with lettuce or doilies work well for small or large serving platters.

Hollowed out loaves of bread work well for dips and spreads. Do not fill too far in advance or the bread will get soggy.

Large hollowed out vegetables like pumpkins or squash can be used for soups, vegetable bowls, sauce containers, etc.

Hollowed out watermelon or cantelope make an attractive fruit or salad bowl. Choose sizes and colors to match your event.

Baskets of all sizes and shapes are available at low costs. Use various baskets for food platters, flower containers, candle holders, bread holders, utensil containers, table decorations, etc.

New flat sheets work well as table coverings, especially outdoors. You might want to tack down the edges of the sheet if the wind is blowing, but do not drive nails or staples into fabric if you plan to use the sheet again.

Ice carving molds are available at restaurant supply businesses. With a little practice you can have a very elegant decorating item. Make sure you have an adequate pan under the carving to catch the melting ice.

Cake decorating shops carry all types of books of interest to the entertainer. You can also take cake decorating classes for a very low price, considering what you learn.

Party supply stores have paper streamers and decorating items of all styles and sizes. These stores are listed in the yellow pages of your phone book.

Framed mirrors make dazzling serving platters. Clean the mirror well and decorate with small candles for a sparkling effect.

Sometimes it is possible to rent plants for large events. You will need to do some research to find a business that will rent to the public.

Color can sometimes liven up a drab office or rented hall. Paper and plastic supplies are available in all colors.

Disposable items are available for almost any serving need i.e., napkins, plates, cups, glasses, utensils, ashtrays, tablecloths, trays, etc.

Decorate a small square basket with flowers. Attach helium balloons to give the affect of a hot-air balloon. Small helium tanks will fill 100 balloons.

Rental Items

Supplies are usually of two types, purchased or rented. Paper and plastic or styrofoam products such as napkins, plates, glasses, flatware and table coverings can be purchased at rental supply stores.

Visit a rental supply store that has a display room so you can see what types of supplies are available in your area. Rented items are listed in catalogues available in your area. You will usually find everthing you could need for your particular event. Many supply businesses deliver for a small charge or you can pick your items up yourself and return them the next day.

Ask your caterer to include the cost of rental items in the overall bill. Most caterers have these items readily available for use. Ask what the difference in cost for such items will be. You will be able to decide whether it will be less expensive if you supplied the items yourself.

Some halls or private clubs will let you use the supplies in their kitchens. You may have to pay a small fee or this may be included in the total cost. Read your contract carefully; you may be charged for breakage.

The following list of rental items is to give you an estimate of what rental businesses charge for these items. Prices will vary from city-to-city. The deposits required will depend on items rented and length of use. You will be charged for breakage. Read your contract carefully for additional details.

Rental Item List

Tables (each)
Banquet, 6' or 8' . . . . $ 6.50
Card or cocktail . . . . $ 5.50
Round, 5', 6' or 8' . . . . $ 6-$8
Umbrella tables . . . . $ 15.00

Chairs (each)
Folding, not padded . . . . $ .75
Stack, padded . . . . $ 1.25
Wood, folding . . . . $ 1.25

Beverage Fountains (each)
Silver, 2½-5 gal . . . . $ 25.00
Gold, 2½-5 gal . . . . $ 25.00
Matching tray . . . . $ 12.50
Silverplate, 3 gal . . . . $ 45.00

Coffee Makers (each)
30-cup . . . . $ 7.50
50-cup . . . . $ 9.00
100-cup . . . . $ 10.00

Canopies (each)
Tie-down 10'x10' . . . . $ 35.00
Free-standing:
10'x10' . . . . $ 80.00
12'x12' . . . . $ 90.00
15'x15' $100.00
20'x20' $140.00
Sides for canopy, 15' . . . . . . $ 8.00

Silver Holloware (each)
Silver service - 5 piece . . . . . . $ 30.00
Coffee of tea server . . . . $ 6.50
Sugar bowl or creamer . . . . . . $ 3.00
Silver trays . . . . $ 8-$15
Coffee urns:
15-cup . . . . $ 30.00
25-cup . . . . $ 40.00
50-cup . . . . $ 50.00
Chafing dish-3 qt. . . . . $ 25.00
Toasting goblets - pair . . . . . . $ 5.00
Nut dish . . . . $ 3.50
Cake knife and server . . . . . . $ 5.00
Wine or Champagne cooler . . . $ 7.00

Rental Items (Continued)

China (each)
Dinner plate, 10"	$ .20
Luncheon plate, 9"	$ .20
Salad plate, 7¼"	$ .20
Saucer, 6"	$ .20
Bread and Butter plate, 6"	$ .20

Flatware - stainless (each)
Dinner knives and forks	$ .18
Salad forks	$ .18
Teaspoons, tablespoons and soup spoons	$ .18
Serving spoons and forks	$ .75

Flatware - silverplate (each)
Dinner knives and forks	$ .30
Salad forks	$ .30
Teaspoons, tablespoons and soup spoons	$ .30
Serving spoons and forks	$ 2.25

Serving Accessories (each)
Chafing Dish - sterno heat:	
Full Size	$ 13.50
Half Size	$ 8.00
Pans: For chafing dishes above	
21"x12"x2½"	$ 2.50
21"x12"x4"	$ 2.50
12"x10"x2½"	$ 1.50
12"x10"x4"	$ 1.50
Heat Lamps	$ 12.00
Hot trays:	
11"x19"	$ 7.00
13"x24"	$ 10.00
Plastic trays & bowls:	
12"x16"	$ 3.00
16"x22"	$ 3.00
16" round	$ 3.00
11", 16", 18" bowls	$ 3.00
Salad Bar	$ 18.00
Stainless Steel Trays and Bowls:	
20" round or 20" oblong	$ 5.00
25" round tray	$ 7.00
2-tier, 25" high	$ 13.00
Stainless wine cooler with stand	$ 8.00
Waiter tray	$ 4.00
Steam Tables	$20-$50
Stockpots:	
5 gallon	$ 5.00
10 gallon	$ 7.00
Propane Hotplates	$20-$30
Barbecues, 5'x2'	$30-$50

Glassware (each)
Snack set-cup and tray	$ .35
Dinner or luncheon plate	$ .20
Salad, bread and butter	$ .20
Coffee or tea cup	$ .20
Saucer	$ .20
Salad bowl, 10'	$ 2.75
Salad bowl, 2½ gal.	$ 6.00
Salt and pepper shakers	$ .50
Coffee mugs, white	$ .18

Glasses and Stemware (each)
Beer mugs	$ .20
Irish Coffe mugs	$ .20
Glasses:	
Hi-ball, 6 or 8 oz.	$ .18
Cordial, 1½ oz.	$ .18
Old Fashioned, 7 oz.	$ .18
Old Fashioned, 12 oz.	$ .18
Shot Glass, 1 oz	$ .18
Water, 10 or 12 oz.	$ .18
Water goblet	$ .20
Stemware:	
Brandy snifter	$ .22
Champagne, 4½ oz	$ .22
Cocktail, 3½ oz	$ .22
Pilsner, 10 oz	$ .22
Tulip Champagne, 6 oz	$ .22
Wine, 6 or 8 oz	$ .22
Margarita	$ .22

Table Linens (each)
Banquet, 54"x120"	$ 7.00
Round, 90"	$ 7.00
Lace cloths	$ 7.00
Card table cloths	$ 5.00
Dinner napkins	$ .50

Punch Bowls (each)
2-2½ gal. 64-80 cup	$ 7.00
3 gal., 96 cup	$ 8.00
Silver, w/ornate ladle	$ 15.00
Gold, w/ladle	$ 15.00
Stainless steel, 7 gal.	$ 13.00

Miscellaneous (each)
Portable bar	$10-$20
P.A. system	$ 25.00
Dance floor:	
3'x3' Parquet sections	$ 7.00
Beer keg tap	$ 5.50
Beer keg container	$ 10.00
Helium tanks	$25-$75

Staff

Staff members vary in fees they charge. The fee will depend on what their duties are and their expertise. Servers or helpers will charge between $5.00 to $12.00 per hour. Independent bartenders usually charge from $7.00 to $15.00 per hour, depending on duties. This is something you need to decide in advance. Outline all duties required of them before the function is underway.

Professional bartending services charge between $20.00 to $30.00 per hour for each bartender. Charges will depend on duties required of each bartender.

One way to cut cost is to have friends or relatives help in serving and/or the preparation of your function. Do not let your friends or relatives get stuck working the whole party; it is better to have several hired staff members in addition to volunteers.

Find out in advance whether your friends or relatives are qualified to handle a particular job. Outlining duties in advance saves time and makes things run more smoothly.

Caterers will be happy to supply servers or bartenders for your event. The price will vary depending on duties and expertise. Check with restaurants and other businesses for available staff members. Always ask the charges in advance. Check the contract to make sure all charges are clearly stated.

The following chart will help you determine how many staff members you will need for your event. Some events will require fewer staff members than stated and others will require more. You will have to make this judgement based on your particular event. When in doubt, have one extra person standing by in case they are needed.

How Many Staff Members

Buffet style	1 server for each 25-40 guests
Sit-down style	1 server for each 12-15 guests
Bussers	1 for each 25-50 guests
Hors d'oeuvre or cocktail style	1 server for each 35-50 guests
Bartenders	1 for each 50-75 guests
Kitchen helpers	1 for each 100 guests
Coffee servers	1 server for each 75 guests
Punch servers	1 server for each 75 guests
Cake servers	1 server for each 50-75 guests
Clean-up helpers	2-4 after a large event, 1-2 for clean-up the following day, check your contract for requirements

CHAPTER 9

PHOTOGRAPHER
TRANSPORTATION
ENTERTAINMENT

Always require references when hiring photographers, chauffeurs, entertainers and other professionals.

Read all contracts carefully before signing them. It is important to investigate all charges and conditions before you commit yourself verbally or in writing. Ask questions and make sure you know all about the contract and the people you will be hiring.

Photographer

Photographers are usually hired for weddings and wedding receptions. If you are having a wedding and want to do something different, consider a video tape. If you check around you might be able to find someone who will do this job for a reasonable rate.

If you should decide to hire a photographer, ask friends and relatives for recommendations. You may have a friend who is an amateur photographer and would be willing to take pictures of your event for a small fee or merely for the experience.

Transportation

You will find limosine service available in almost every city. You may be able to cut the cost by asking a friend who owns a classic or antique car to provide you with transportation. Some larger cities have horse and carriage service available.

If you have out of town guests who are staying in various hotels, you might consider having a rental bus pick up the guests at their hotels and take them to the event. You could schedule the bus to take the guests home (back to hotels) at various times during the evening.

Entertainment

Live music is a nice touch for any function, but there is a large cost to consider. You can call local agencies to see what is available in your area and what the cost might be for the type of entertaiment you have in mind.

You may find a friend or relative who knows someone in the music business who would give you a reasonable rate. When cost is a factor, consider taped or stereo music. Some people will bring large music systems and records to a function and act as a disc jockey for less than a group or band might cost.

It is important to investigate the entertainers before hiring them. You do not want to be disappointed with the music during your event. Many times you can hear a tape of an entertainer's music or you can go to a rehearsal and meet the people in person. If you contact a good musical agency you should be able to get the expertise you desire.

CHAPTER 10

RECORD KEEPING
PROLOGUE
BOOK ORDER FORM

Keep your notes orderly and up to date. Make notations to identify certain information. There is nothing worse than finding a small piece of paper with only a phone number on it.

Order additional copies of "A Guide to Catering" as gifts for friends and relatives. This book makes an excellent wedding gift.

Record Keeping

Lists are very important in planning and completing a function. The following form will help you organize collected information. A well planned and organized event will pay for itself many times over.

You may want to type your notes on 8½ by 11-inch sheets of paper and have them added to the back of this book. Simply call a local printer and ask if they have a "plastic comb binding machine". If so, your pages can be punched and added to the book for a small fee.

Record Keeping Form
Phone Numbers • Addresses • Contact Persons

Caterers:

Name _____

Phone _____

Address _____

Contact _____

Name _____

Phone _____

Address _____

Contact _____

Grocery Store:

Name _____

Phone _____

Address _____

Contact _____

Specialty or Wholesale Store:

Name _____

Phone _____

Address _____

Contact _____

Florist:
- Name _____
- Phone _____
- Address _____
- Contact _____

Baker:
- Name _____
- Phone _____
- Address _____
- Contact _____

Printer:
- Name _____
- Phone _____
- Address _____
- Contact _____

Rental Hall & Facilities:
- Name _____
- Phone _____
- Address _____
- Contact _____

Restaurants:
- Name _____
- Phone _____
- Address _____
- Contact _____

Rental Companies & Party Supply Stores:
- Name _____
- Phone _____
- Address _____
- Contact _____

Staff Members:

Name _____

Phone _____

Address _____

Remarks: _____

Name _____

Phone _____

Address _____

Remarks: _____

Others:

Name _____

Phone _____

Address _____

Contact _____

Name _____

Phone _____

Address _____

Contact _____

Name _____

Phone _____

Address _____

Contact _____

NOTES:

_____

_____

_____

_____

_____

_____

_____

_____

_____

Planning Information

Type of event: _____ **Date:** _____ **Time:** _____

Location: _____ **Number of Guests:** _____

Menu:
_____
_____
_____

Beverage: _____
_____

Supplies: _____
_____

Staff: _____
_____
_____

Guest List: _____
_____
_____
_____
_____
_____
_____

NOTES: _____
_____
_____
_____
_____
_____
_____

Prologue

After reading this book you should have a good idea of how the catering business works. Regardless of how you plan to use this information, keep it handy for future reference.

Never be afraid to take on an entertaining challenge. Most people have the ability, but lack the knowledge to successfully cater an event. I hope this information will help you and I sincerely wish you luck in all your endeavors.

If you would like to receive information on lecture tours and fee schedules, please contact:

DJ's Guides
Publicity Dept.
P.O. Box 06472
Portland, OR 97206

Index

Almond Cheese Salad, 51
Anniversary, 14
Appetizers
   Baked Salmon, 42
   Barbecued Pork w/Dipping
     Sauce, 46
   Barbecued Prawns, 41
   Cheese Tray, 37
   Chicken w/ Bearnaise Sauce, 44
   Chicken Liver Pâté, 43
   Chicken & Pork Pâté, 45
   Chicken Wings w/Mustard, 44
   Cocktail Puffs w/Filling, 40
   Cocktail Quiche, 39
   Crab Dip, 37
   Crab & Swiss on Sourdough, 37
   Crispy Chicken Wings, 45
   Dolmates, 48
   Fresh Mushroom Dip, 34
   Fruit Tray, 40
   Guacomole, 38
   Hot Crab Dip, 36
   Macadamia Prawns, 41
   Meatballs, 36
   Mexican Platter, 38
   Pasta Shells w/Bearnaise
     Sauce, 40
   Pot Stickers, 47
   Rumaki, 43
   Salmon Spread, 42
   Spinach Balls, 35
   Spinach Dip, 36
   Spinach & Cheese Filo
     Pastries, 35
   Stuffed Mushrooms, 34
Avocado
   Guacomole, 38
   Mexican Platter, 38
Baked Salmon, 42
Banana Nut Cake, 66
Bar Set-up, 85
Barbecue, 16
Barbecued Pork w/Dipping
  Sauce, 46
Barbecued Prawns, 41
Barbecued Spareribs, 61
Bartenders, 77, 85, 91
Beans
   Green Beans w/Waterchestnuts, 54
Bearnaise Sauce, 44
Beef
   Beef Burgundy, 59
   Mexican Platter, 38
   Meatballs, 36

Beverage
   Bar Set-up, 85
   Beverage Quantities, 85
   Wine Terminology, 79-80
   Grape Variety, 81-83
   <u>See</u> Punches & Drinks
Beverage Quantities
   Champagne, 85
   Coffee, 85
   Liquor & Mixers, 85
   Punch, 85
Birthday, 14
Biscuits
   Small Biscuits, 68
Bleu Cheese Onions, 54
Book Order Forms, 100
Breads
   Bran Muffins, 69
   Brunch Rolls, 69
   Garlic Bread, 71
   Gingerbread, 67
   Small Bisquits, 68
Brocolli w/Bacon & Almonds, 56
Budget, 25
Buffett Potatoes, 55
Cake
   Cutting, 20
   Gingerbread, 67
   Sizes, 20
   Sour Cream Breakfast Cake, 68
Cappuccino, 71
Carrots
   Gingered Carrots, 54
Catering Costs, 29-32
Champagne Punch, 72
Cheese
   Almond Cheese Salad, 51
   Bleu Cheese Onions, 54
   Buffet Potatoes, 55
   Cheese & Egg Scramble, 64
   Cheese Tray, 37
   Chicken & Crab Kiev w/Gruyere
     Cheese Sauce, 60
   Cocktail Quiche, 39
   Crab & Swiss on Sourdough, 37
   Cream of Spinach Soup
     w/Cheese, 49
   Mexican Platter, 38
   Mushroom, Bleu Cheese &
     Walnut Salad, 52
   Spinach Balls, 35
   Spinach & Cheese Filo Pastries, 35
   Spinach Lasagne, 62
   Stuffed Mushrooms, 34

Cheese (Continued)
    Tomato and Pepper Salad w/Bleu
        Cheese Dressing, 52
    Vegetable Casserole, 57
Chicken
    Chicken w/Bearnaise Sauce, 44
    Chicken & Crab Kiev w/Gruyere
        Cheese Sauce, 60
    Chicken Liver Pâté, 43
    Chicken & Pork Pâté, 45
    Chicken Wings w/Dijon Mustard, 44
    Chinese Chicken Salad, 51
    Epicurean Chicken Livers, 59
Church, 15
Chinese Chicken Salad, 51
Chocolate
    Chocolate Eggnog, 72
    Creamed Chocolate, 70
    Macadamia Nut Fudge, 65
Clams w/Wine, 61
Cocktail Puffs w/Filling, 40
Cocktail Quiche, 39
Cookies
    Madeleines, 65
Costs
    Facility, 25-26
    Food and Catering, 29-32
    Gratuities, 25-26
    Rental Items, 89-90
Costume, 16
Crab
    Chicken & Crab Kiev w/Gruyere
        Cheese Sauce, 60
    Crab Dip, 37
    Crab & Swiss on Sourdough, 37
    Hot Crab Dip, 36
Cranberries
    Orange Cranberry Sauce, 70
Cream of Spinach Soup w/Cheese, 49
Creamed Chocolate, 70
Creamed Tomato Sauce, 62
Crispy Chicken Wings, 45
Curry Powders, 73
Decorating & Serving Suggestions, 88
Decorations, 87-88
Desserts
    Banana Nut Cake, 66
    Bran Muffins, 69
    Brunch Rolls, 69
    Creamed Chocolate, 70
    French Vanilla Ice Cream
        w/Grand Marnier, 65
    Gingerbread, 67
    Macadamia Nut Fudge, 65
    Madeleines, 65
    Orange Cranberry Sauce, 70
    Pumpkin Rum Mousse, 67
    Small Bisquits, 68
    Sherbet & Champagne, 70
    Sour Cream Breakfast Cake, 68
Dinner, 16
Dipping Sauce for Barbecued
    Pork, 46
Dolmates, 48
Easy French Toast, 64
Easy Mulled Punch, 71
Egg
    Cheese & Egg Scramble, 64
    Chocolate Eggnog, 72
Entertainment, 93
Entrées See Main Dishes
Epicurean Chicken Livers, 59
Facility, 25-26
Filling for Cocktail Puffs or
    Pasta Shells w/Bearnaise Sauce, 40
Five Spice Powder, 73
Freezer Storage, 75
French Onion Soup, 50
French Toast, 64
French Vanilla Ice Cream
    w/Grand Marnier, 65
Fruit Tray, 40
Garlic Bread, 71
Gingerbread, 67
Gingered Carrots, 54
Glazed Ham & Sausage, 58
Graduation, 14
Grape Name & Area, 78
Grape Variety, 81-83
Gruyere Cheese Sauce, 60
Guacomole, 38
Halls & Auditoriums, 26
Ham
    Glazed Ham & Sausage, 58
Health
    Hints for the Healthy, 74
Hot Crab Dip, 36
Hot Mustard Sauce for
    Barbecued Pork, 46
How to Use This Book, 7
Ice Cream
    French Vanilla Ice Cream
        w/Grand Marnier, 65
    Vanilla Ice Cream w/Orange
        Cranberry Sauce, 70

Introduction, 7
Invitations, 87
Kitchen Help, 91
Lamb
   Dolmates, 48
   Lamb w/Rosemary Stuffing
     and Mustard Sauce, 58
Lasagne
   Spinach Lasagne, 62
Leek Soup, 50
Liquor Quantities, 85
Macadamia Nut Fudge, 65
Macadamia Prawns, 41
Madeleines, 65
Main Dishes
   Baked Clams w/Wine, 61
   Barbecued Spareribs, 61
   Beef Burgundy, 59
   Cheese & Egg Scramble, 64
   Chicken & Crab Kiev w/Gruyere
     Cheese Sauce, 60
   Easy French Toast, 64
   Epicurean Chicken Livers, 59
   Glazed Ham & Sausage, 58
   Lamb w/Rosemary and Mustard
     Sauce, 58
   Spaghetti Sauce, 63
   Spinach Lasagne, 62
Meatballs, 36
Menus
   Buffet Brunch, 30
   Buffet or Sit Down Dinner, 31
   Buffet or Sit Down Luncheon, 30
   Hors d'oeuvre Style, 29-30
   Large Feast or Fund Raiser, 32
   Picnic, Barbecue or Pot Luck, 31
   Sit Down Dinner, 31
   Wine Tasting, 30
Mexican Platter, 38
Mixer Quantities, 85
Muffins
   Bran Muffins, 69
Mushrooms
   Fresh Mushroom Dip, 34
   Mushroom, Bleu Cheese & Walnut
     Salad, 52
   Mushrooms w/Herbs, 59
   Shrimp Salad w/Mushrooms, 53
   Stuffed Mushrooms, 34
Number of Guests, 14
Onions
   Bleu Cheese Onions, 54
Open House
   Office, 15
   Home, 15

Orange Cranberry Sauce, 70
Oriental Soup, 49
Outline
   Planning a Function, 9-12
Party, 14
Pasta
   Spaghetti Sauce, 63
   Spinach Lasagne, 62
Pâté
   Chicken Liver Pâté, 43
   Pork & Chicken Pâté, 45
Photographer, 93
Picnic, 16
Planning Information Form, 98
Pork
   Barbecued Pork w/Dipping Sauce, 46
   Barbecued Spareribs, 61
   Glazed Ham & Sausage, 58
   Pot Stickers, 47
Pot Stickers, 47
Potatoes
   Buffet Potatoes, 55
Prawns
   Barbecued Prawns, 41
   Macadamia Prawns, 41
   Shrimp Salad w/Mushrooms, 53
Preface, 6
Prologue, 99
Pumpkin Rum Mousse, 67
Punches & Drinks
   Cappuccino, 71
   Champagne Punch, 72
   Chocolate Eggnog, 72
   Easy Mulled Punch, 71
   Milk Punch, 71
   Waikiki Punch, 72
Questions
   Special Request Address, 99
Recipes
   Appetizers, 34-48
   Desserts, 65-73
   Main Dishes, 58-64
   Punches & Misc., 65-73
   Soups & Salads, 49-53
   Vegetables & Side Dishes, 54-57
Recipe Symbols, 29
Record Keeping Form, 95-97
Rental Items, 89-90
Reunions
   Family, 15
   School, 15
Rice
   Rice Pilaf, 56

Rolls
    Bran Muffins, 69
    Brunch Rolls, 69
R.S.V.P., 13-14
Rumaki, 43
Salads
    Almond Cheese Salad, 51
    Chinese Chicken Salad, 51
    Mushroom, Bleu Cheese
        & Walnut Salad, 52
    Tomato & Pepper w/Bleu
        Cheese Salad, 52
    Shrimp w/Mushroom Salad, 53
Salmon
    Baked Salmon, 42
    Salmon Spread, 42
Sauces
    Bearnaise Sauce, 44
    Creamed Tomato Sauce, 62
    Gruyere Cheese Sauce, 62
    Orange Cranberry Sauce, 70
    Spaghetti Sauce, 63
Sausage
    Glazed Ham & Sausage, 58
Seafood
    Barbecued Prawns, 41
    Clams w/Wine, 61
    Chicken & Crab Kiev w/Gruyere
        Cheese Sauce, 60
    Crab Dip, 37
    Crab & Swiss on Sourdough, 37
    Hot Crab Dip, 36
    Macadamia Prawns, 41
    Shrimp Salad w/Mushrooms, 53
Servers
    Staff, 91
Set-up, 22
Sherbet & Champagne, 70
Shrimp Salad w/Mushrooms, 53
Soups
    Cream of Spinach w/Cheese Soup, 49
    French Onion Soup, 50
    Leek Soup, 50
    Oriental Soup, 49
Spaghetti Sauce, 63
Spices
    Five Spice Powder, 73
    Hot Curry, 73
    Mild Curry, 73
Spinach
    Spinach Balls, 35
    Spinach & Cheese Filo Pastries, 35
    Spinach Dip, 36
    Spinach Lasagne, 62

Spreads
    Cocktail Puff Filling, 40
    Liver Pâté, 43
    Salmon Spread, 42
    Spinach Dip, 36
Staff
    Wages, 91
    Number Needed, 91
Stuffed Mushrooms, 34
Style, 23
Table of Contents, 4-5
Tomatoes
    Creamed Tomato Sauce, 62
    Tomato & Pepper w/Bleu Cheese
        Salad, 52
    Tomato Timbles, 55
Transportation, 93
Type of Function, 14-16
Vegetables & Side Dishes
    Bleu Cheese Onions, 54
    Brocolli w/Bacon & Almonds, 56
    Buffet Potatoes, 55
    Gingered Carrots, 54
    Green Beans w/Waterchestnuts, **54**
    Mushrooms w/Herbs, **59**
    Rice Pilaf, **56**
    Tomato Timbles, **55**
    Vegetable Casserole, **57**
Videotape, 93
Wages & Fees
    Bartenders, 77, 91
    Servers & Helpers, 91
Wedding Reception, 16
Wedding Schedule, 17-18
Wedding Section
    Cakes: How to cut, 20
    Wedding Schedule, 17-18
    Who Pays?, 19
Wine
    Grape Names & Areas, 78
    Grape Variety, 81-83
    How Much Champagne, **85**
    Where to Buy Wines, 84
    Wine Terminology, 79-80

Donna Miller has been in the food service industry for twenty years. She owns and operates a catering business and cooking school, Epicurean Delight, in Portland, Oregon.

Due to her success in business and teaching she has been asked to appear on numerous television and radio programs. Reviewers have hailed "A Guide to Catering" as one of the best works dealing with the problems and solutions of catering and entertaining.

Solve the following addition problems:

```
  2        2        4        6        4
+ 6      + 4      + 3      + 1      + 2
___      ___      ___      ___      ___
[ ]      [ ]      [ ]      [ ]      [ ]


  5        3        2        4        5
+ 3      + 2      + 3      + 4      + 0
___      ___      ___      ___      ___
[ ]      [ ]      [ ]      [ ]      [ ]
```

Addition Doubles: Add and write the sums.

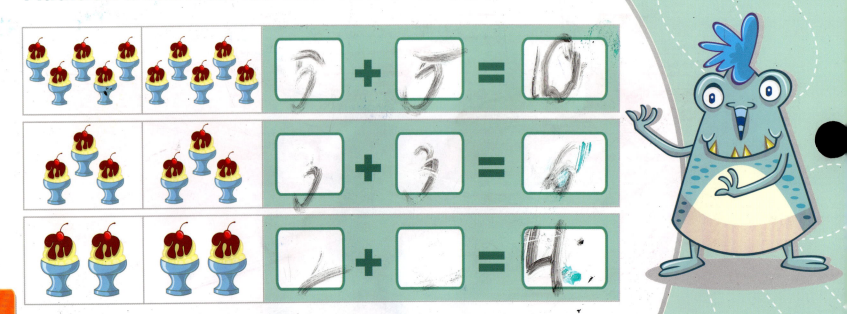

Count the cherries and write the sums.

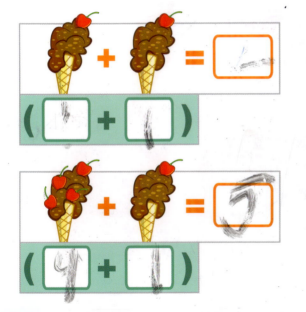
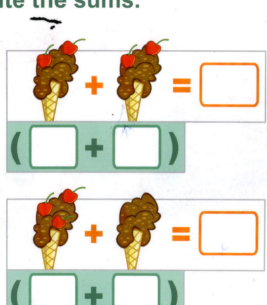

Write the number that completes the sum.

1 + ☐ = 5   4 + ☐ = 8

5 + ☐ = 8   6 + ☐ = 9

3 + ☐ = 6   2 + ☐ = 4

Count the apples and add them together.

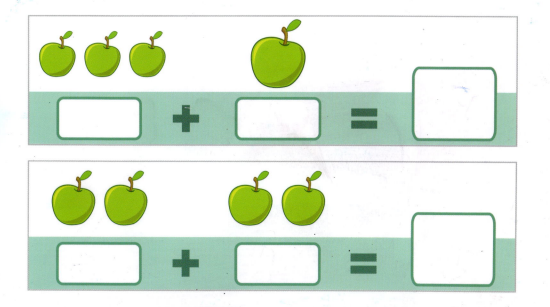

Addition Doubles: Add and write the sums.

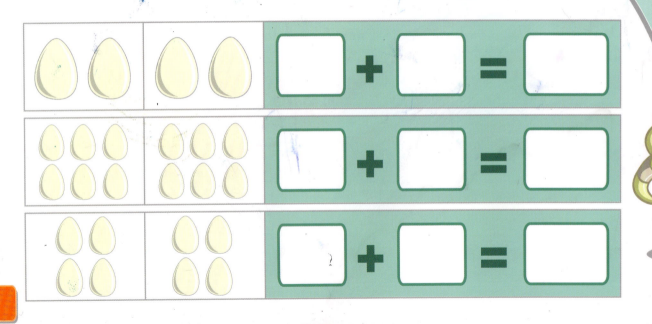

Solve the following addition problems:

```
  5      6      3      4      5
+ 2    + 2    + 4    + 1    + 4
───    ───    ───    ───    ───
[  ]   [  ]   [  ]   [  ]   [  ]

  3      2      4      6      8
+ 2    + 5    + 3    + 4    + 1
───    ───    ───    ───    ───
[  ]   [  ]   [  ]   [  ]   [  ]
```

Count the cherries and add them together.

Count the pepperoni pieces and write the sums.

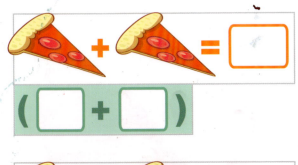
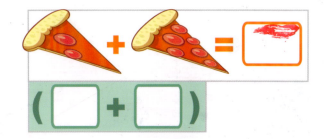
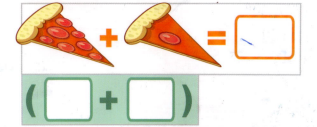
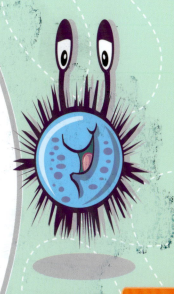

Write the number that completes the sum.

$0 + \boxed{} = 5$ $\qquad$ $1 + \boxed{} = 2$

$3 + \boxed{} = 7$ $\qquad$ $4 + \boxed{} = 9$

$6 + \boxed{} = 6$ $\qquad$ $3 + \boxed{} = 4$

Write the number that completes the sum.

7 + ☐ = 7   5 + ☐ = 9

2 + ☐ = 8   1 + ☐ = 6

1 + ☐ = 3   2 + ☐ = 7

Solve the following addition problems:

$$\begin{array}{r}9\\+\ 1\\\hline\end{array}\qquad\begin{array}{r}2\\+\ 6\\\hline\end{array}\qquad\begin{array}{r}1\\+\ 8\\\hline\end{array}\qquad\begin{array}{r}2\\+\ 0\\\hline\end{array}\qquad\begin{array}{r}5\\+\ 3\\\hline\end{array}$$

$$\begin{array}{r}2\\+\ 2\\\hline\end{array}\qquad\begin{array}{r}1\\+\ 1\\\hline\end{array}\qquad\begin{array}{r}7\\+\ 4\\\hline\end{array}\qquad\begin{array}{r}6\\+\ 4\\\hline\end{array}\qquad\begin{array}{r}1\\+\ 6\\\hline\end{array}$$

Addition Doubles: Add and write the sums.

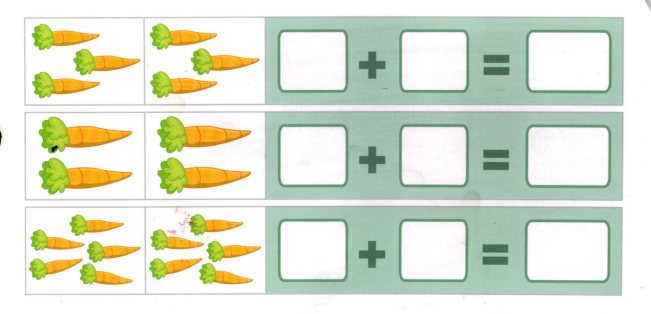

Count the French fries and write the sums.

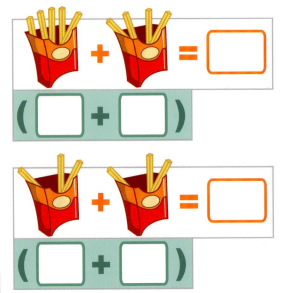
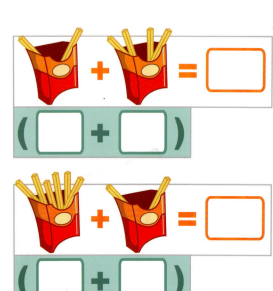
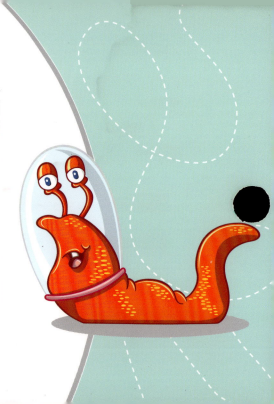

Addition Doubles: Add and write the sums.

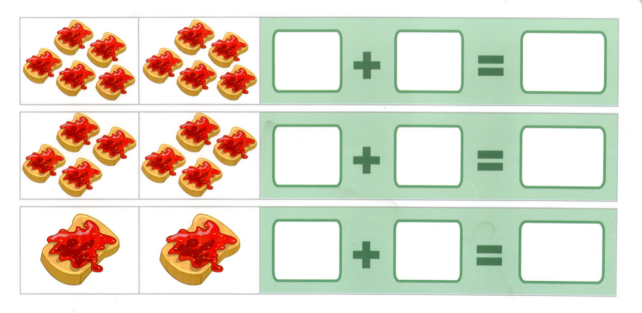

Count the oranges and add them together.

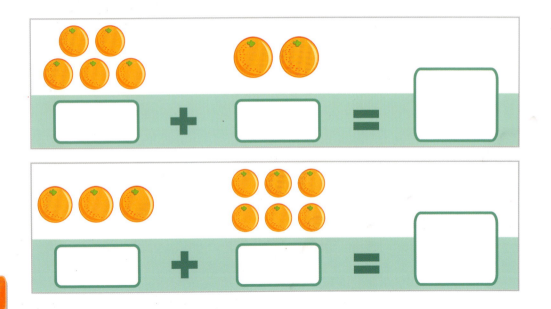

Solve the following addition problems:

```
  6      3      9      2      6
+ 3    + 5    + 1    + 7    + 6
───    ───    ───    ───    ───
[ ]    [ ]    [ ]    [ ]    [ ]


  5      1      3      4      3
+ 5    + 2    + 0    + 6    + 9
───    ───    ───    ───    ───
[ ]    [ ]    [ ]    [ ]    [ ]
```

Addition Doubles: Add and write the sums.

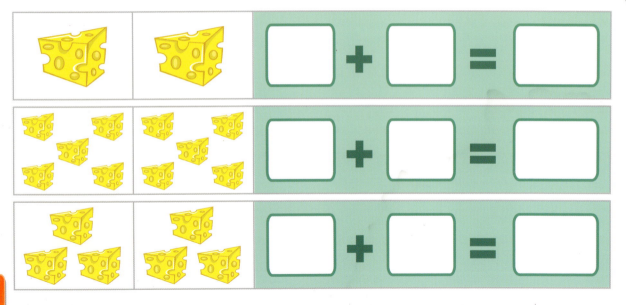
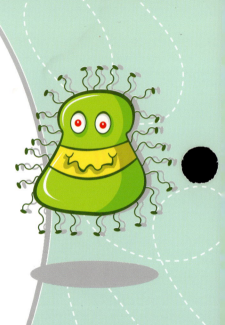

Count the bananas and add them together.

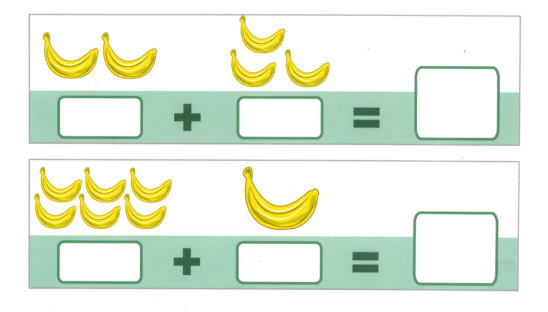

Solve the following addition problems:

```
  8      3      1      1      7
+ 0    + 3    + 4    + 5    + 0
___    ___    ___    ___    ___
[ ]    [ ]    [ ]    [ ]    [ ]


  1      5      6      3      1
+ 7    + 1    + 0    + 5    + 6
___    ___    ___    ___    ___
[ ]    [ ]    [ ]    [ ]    [ ]
```

Count the apples and add them together.

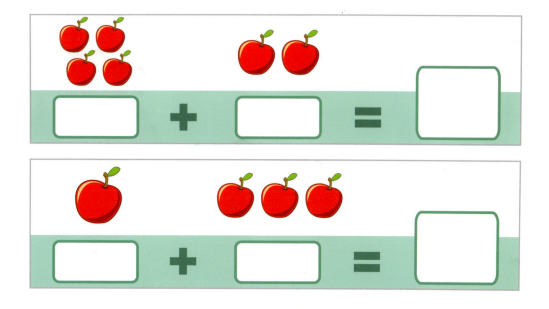

Addition Doubles: Add and write the sums.

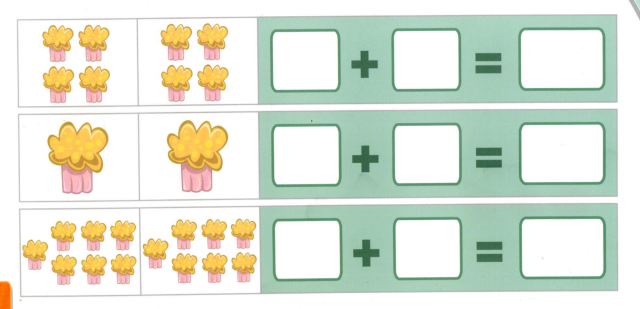

Write the number that completes the sum.

5 + ☐ = 7   2 + ☐ = 6

1 + ☐ = 4   3 + ☐ = 5

6 + ☐ = 7   4 + ☐ = 4

Count the chocolate chips and write the sums.

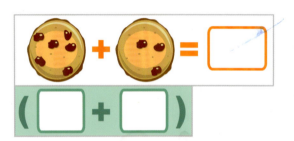